100

THINGS TO DO IN
PORTLAND
MAINE
BEFORE YOU
DIE

For my aunt Karen Stephens.

Your encouragement, unconditional love, and support
has given me the courage to fearlessly pursue a creative life.
I owe you so much more than these words.

And for my daughters, Samantha and Alexandra.

It is not an accident that you grew up in this marvelous city.
Sharing Portland with you makes discovering new things—and
rediscovering old ones—magical for me!

100

THINGS TO DO IN PORTLAND MAINE BEFORE YOU DIE

• •

ROBERT WITKOWSKI

REEDY PRESS

Library of Congress Control Number: 2015930928

ISBN: 9781935806974

Design by Jill Halpin

Cover Photo: Kim Seng

Printed in the United States of America
15 16 17 18 19   5 4 3 2 1

Please note that websites, phone numbers, addresses, and company names are subject to change or cancellation. We did our best to relay the most accurate information available, but due to circumstances beyond our control, please do not hold us liable for misinformation. When exploring new destinations, please do your homework before you go.

CONTENTS

• •

• •

• •

PREFACE

It is no accident that I live in Portland, Maine. Portland is not for everyone. It's not enough that you want to be here. Portland has to want you to be here too. The longer I stay, the more the people of Maine open up, and the more I learn about this wonderfully interesting and fun city!

When approached to select 100 life-worthy things to do in Portland, I thought it would be easy to compile. My preliminary list was way more than 100. Cuts needed to be made. This was neither easy nor expected. The process presented very difficult choices I was not prepared to make.

These 100 selections are not related to my role at the Convention and Visitors Bureau. They were chosen from my personal criteria derived from my experiences in Portland over the past decade. Each of the final 100 Things to Do is selected based on its own merit, within the following criteria (which still required cutting!):

- Within Portland city limits (there are a few exceptions, but they snuck in by having Portland-based transportation and extraordinary iconic relevance to Portland).
- Uniqueness and/or significance in the city
- Something the general public can do
- Things I personally experienced as a participant or spectator. In a few cases I extensively interviewed those who could convey it effectively and accurately.
- I attempted to avoid duplication, so while there may be many extraordinary places that do similar things, I singled out those I determined to be the worthiest of the list.
- Items selected need to be well established or, if recently established, demonstrate staying power with a commitment from organizers for a reliable future.

The end result surprised even me. I was struck by the cross section of the final 100. With Portland increasingly recognized as a culinary destination, starting with being named America's Foodiest Small Town by *Bon Appetite* magazine as far back as 2009, it wasn't a shock that Food and Drink stood above the other sections. What caught me off guard was who made the cut. For all the fine dining and outstanding chefs, much of the section comprises food and eateries that are quirky, and all Portland. Those aspects seem to permeate the book as a whole.

As in most cities, things change, places close, and (as the title indicates) people die. Apologies in advance if anything in this list is unexpectedly altered or nonexistent by the time you get to the door. Send me an email and I will provide an alternative (rtwitkowski@gmail.com).

Furthermore, if the information provided is in some way inaccurate, dated, misspelled, or just plain wrong, I beg forgiveness. I have made every effort to get it right, but research can be flawed, people have revisionist history, and information may be misinterpreted. If that occurs, I apologize.

If any who've made this list take my attempts at humor as insulting, don't be silly! What's most compelling and enjoyable about many of the entries is the no-nonsense or grittiness that is Maine. I bring attention to these elements not to offend, but to make unsuspecting readers aware of what to expect. The goal is to not have a newbie venture somewhere and be caught off guard, have a terrible time, and believe the list is flawed.

Please know that if you are on this list, or quoted in it, the reason is because I believe you to be one of the best things to do in Portland! I cannot possibly mean insult or harm because I truly believe you're offering something fulfilling in life—go with that!

The other side of that coin is that just because you aren't on the list doesn't mean you aren't awesome too! Maybe you're just number 101. I am aware that I may get berated by friends and associates who may demand to know why they didn't make the book. The reason is that I even had to cut a few of my personal favorites! It's just that I needed to stop at 100.

Portland and the surrounding metropolitan region is one of the greatest urban areas to live in this country. Why else would I choose this seaside landscape as a home after living in the vibrant cities of Chicago, Boston, and New York? Portland offers much of what is enjoyable about those major metropolitan areas, and almost none of the aggravations.

If I can't show you this city in person, I am honored to be here with you in words. Please enjoy.

• •

ACKNOWLEDGMENTS

I greatly appreciate all the people in my life who supported me in so many ways, whether they knew it or not, in writing this book. It is because of their encouragement, enticements, goading, and simply inviting me to join them in escapades around Portland that I am able to present these 100 things worthy of life. Their love and friendship were critical (literally and figuratively) in my writing this book.

Thanks to Chris Riccardo, Bill Ryan, and Grete Zemans for their time, patience, and honesty in reading—and re-reading—*100 Things to Do in Portland*. Their efforts reading this when it was unreadable will (hopefully) spare me great embarrassment and ensure a (hopefully) fun and informative read.

Deep appreciation for my daughters, Samantha and Alexandra, for suffering through my nights out researching (see, it wasn't all just a lot of fun!), the days out writing, alleviating my concerns, enduring repeated readings out loud, and telling me how great it is with patient eye rolls and forgiving smiles. Gratitude to Craig Barnes who forced me to go out and relax, even though he didn't always know why.

I also thank all the people who trusted me enough to let me in and take the time to speak with me, especially: Kathi Adams, Erica Archer, David Davis, Pam Laskey, Kristen Levesque, Angel Gonzalez Jr., Jen Hale, John Hatcher, Dan Kennedy, Oscar Mokeme, Jeff Peterson, Laura Peterson, Dorinda Putnam, Rash Sandhu, Caitlin Prentice (so *close*), and Chris Riccardo. Hope I did you proud!

Special gratitude to city councilor and former mayor Ed Suslovic. I am humbled that he took valuable time from his schedule to offer a foreword to this book. His dedication to and love for Portland are evident in his contribution, and I'm proud to have his words and friendship.

And a special shout out to Kim Miller for believing this book is a reason to celebrate by tirelessly promoting it through her company. I am forever grateful.

I am deeply appreciative of the jobs and associates who've welcomed me, friends who've made me family, and the city that fits me so well.

FOREWORD

Portland, Maine, and Robert Witkowski—a perfect match!

Let's start with Portland. A city with a big heart, an even bigger appetite, and a presence that burrows deeper and deeper into your heart the longer you live here. Comfortable, casual, yet with the ability to surprise you when you least expect it. Walking the streets of the Old Port or strolling Congress Street on a First Friday Art Walk means running into old friends as well as making new ones. Creative energy pulsing through the veins of her people resulting in colorful bursts of innovation that attract more creative types and . . . well, you get the picture.

Now we come to Robert "Bob" Witkowski. See above. No, really! Bob is the personification of all the best attributes of Longfellow's "City by the Sea." Not only has he become part of Portland's vibe, but he is a major contributor to the vibrancy that has placed Portland on just about every Top Ten list around. Going out to lunch with him means good food, great company, and making new acquaintances, leaving you pleasantly sated gastronomically and socially. Boring is never a word used to describe Bob, since he and his family excel at creating adventure and excitement wherever they explore. As a city councilor who spends too much time in meetings, I get to live vicariously through Bob. Anytime I start to think that I know all that Portland has to offer, Bob sneaks one past me and I'm following his lead on another fascinating adventure.

I know that every reader will want to join me in thanking Bob for showing us parts of Portland unknown to us until now. It takes a curious creativity to ferret out the individual strands of DNA that come together and create this city that never lets us down. Enjoy!

Edward J. Suslovic
—*Maine House of Representatives, District 32, 2002–2004*
—*Mayor of Portland, 2007–2008*
—*Portland City Councilor, At-Large, 2005–2008*
—*Portland City Councilor, District 3, 2010–present*

100

THINGS TO DO IN
PORTLAND
MAINE
BEFORE YOU
DIE

FOOD
AND DRINK

TOAST THE TOWN
FROM TOP OF THE EAST

The Top of the East is the only rooftop bar and gastropub in the city with commanding views of the Portland skyline and harbor. Atop the Westin Portland Harborview Hotel in the Arts District, the cocktail lounge's name is derived from its perch atop the 1927 high-rise originally named the Eastland Park Hotel.

Listed on the National Register of Historic Places, this iconic downtown hotel has famously hosted celebrities from Charles Lindbergh to Julia Roberts—but not First Lady Eleanor Roosevelt . . . she was refused because of her dogs. ("Dogs are now welcomed by the Westin brand," winks GM Bruce Wennerstrom.)

A recent $50 million hotel renovation doubled Top of the East's size. Stunning views of water, woods, and New Hamphire's White Mountains surrounding the Forest City afford a 360-degree panorama. Sunsets give way to the glow of city lights and flashes of the harbor lighthouses. A Dark and Stormy cocktail, anyone?

157 High St.
207-775-5411
westinportlandharborview.com/top-of-the-east

DINE DOCKSIDE
AT DIMILLO'S ON THE WATER

Feast on chowder, fish, and lobster presented in traditional or playful ways, including DiMillo's style lobster mac & cheese and deep-fried lobster tails, while soaking in the sea air on this car-ferry-turned-floating-restaurant docked on the waterfront.

An Old Port institution was dangerously close to being a tourist trap when the second generation of the DiMillo family revamped their namesake restaurant. The most notable change was piping aboard Chef Melissa Bouchard. Her impact is tasted in a culinary approach focusing on accentuating Maine's agriculture and seafood with simply prepared cuisine.

Tony's son, Johnny DiMillo, emphasizes the restaurant's upscale but unpretentious appeal by saying, "We don't cook complicated masterpieces, just good food from fresh ingredients."

In 1982 Tony DiMillo opened New England's only coastal floating restaurant in what had been a seedy red light district in the 1970s. Many regard this as a turning point in Portland's waterfront renaissance. An instant hit when it opened, foodies craving the seaport experience thrill at the innovative renovations that make the ship a fine dining experience. Now, Tony's children and grandchildren literally keep the business afloat.

25 Long Wharf
207-772-2216
dimillos.com/restaurant

Commissioned the *New York* in 1941 as a car ferry, the vessel serviced automobiles crossing the Delaware River, James River (as the *Norfolk*), and Narragansett Bay (as the *Newport*). Tony DiMillo had the hulk redesigned, making the car bay a spacious dining room with cocktail lounge. A portside deck was added later.

• •

Easy parking on Long Wharf.
If you park to shop, plan a quick bite before you leave . . . it's completely free if you validate your parking ticket after eating at DiMillo's on the Water.

GRILLED MUFFIN
AT BECKY'S DINER

There's something about the blueberry muffins toasted on the grill at Becky's Diner that transcends all other muffins. A portside eatery for early-rising fishermen, many nine-to-five suits, and late-night truckers, Becky Rand's "long-running, no-nonsense diner" on Hobson's Wharf has been serving Portland's working waterfront since 1991 with "homemade food for a fair price coming out of our kitchen." Guy Fieri dropped in for an episode of Food Network's *Diners, Drive-Ins, and Dives*. Not to be outdone, Taylor Swift had an after-hours supper with her cast and crew after a long day filming her music video for her song "Mine."

Keeping its reliable commitment of a warm meal waiting for the erratic schedule of the fishing industry, Becky's remains open 362 and a half days a year, 4 a.m.–10 p.m., only closing on Thanksgiving, Christmas Eve night, and Christmas Day.

Make sure to grab a souvenir of your visit: a bumper sticker telling the world, "Becky's Diner—Nuthin' finah"

390 Commercial St.
207-773-7070
beckysdiner.com

Don't mind the line out the door—they're just landlubbers waiting for a table. Excuse yourself past the snarling flatlanders and find an open stool at the counter for immediate service.

ENJOY A FIRST SUPPER
AT GRACE RESTAURANT

Entering Grace Restaurant, hosts greet patrons at a wooden pulpit in the former Chestnut Street United Methodist Church. Guests can opt to enjoy an aperitif in the choir loft above or a drink at the eternal-ring bar in the transept while waiting for a table. Up to one hundred diners bask in the glow of a massive rose window imported from Florence in the mid-1800s. Their meals are expertly crafted in an open kitchen where the altar once stood, appropriately making meals including lamb and fish for supper.

The Gothic church building, adjacent to city hall, was built circa 1856–57 and is one of the only surviving examples of the work of architect Charles Alexander. On the National Register of Historic Places as an early Gothic Revival style in Portland, it's also one of the few structures to survive the Great Fire of 1866, which destroyed two-thirds of the city.

Architect Dean Bingham (who also sidelines as confectionaire extraordinaire owner of Dean's Sweets) presents an innovative vision in this adaptive reuse, which has been wildly popular among foodies since the restaurant's 2009 opening. This unique preservation alone is deserving of gastronomic genuflection.

15 Chestnut St.
207-828-4422
restaurantgrace.com

SHUCK FOR FOOD
AT J'S OYSTER

Taking the cobblestone way past the docked lobster boats behind Commercial Street's curved Thomas Block building, you'll find J's Oyster, a local institution where the regulars will never let you feel like a stranger. The waterfront eatery anchors Long Wharf. Its size is not deceptive—a U-shaped oyster bar fills the single room, leaving little space for the crowd making its way around the joint, being further squeezed by a few tables against the walls.

Don't go for the view. Most seats at J's face inward, and the people come for the bivalve mollusks and the generous pours. Oysters are best in cold water, so the rule of thumb is to eat them in months that have an "R"—September through April. Occasionally stopping in for a nightcap, locals work May through August when J's is invaded by tourists who sit wharfside enjoying Chesapeake Bay–harvested oysters.

Working waterfront nighthawks mix with nearby office sharks to fill J's most any night—kind of a seafood *Cheers*. Walking into the bar can seem intimidating, but by the second round, welcoming banter from any of J's bartenders or expert shuckers will morph into customer cross talk. Before another round, first-timers will feel like family.

5 Portland Pier
207-772-4828

WARM UP AT
GREAT CHILI & CHOWDER CHALLENGE

Every February, Maine's top chefs and restaurants face off with steaming crocks of New England clam chowder, lobster chowder, and chilies. James Beard Award winners pitted against local lobster shacks and family-owned Mexican restaurants often delight foodies and chefs alike with surprises.

This culinary battle in the Arts District is decided by cold and hungry foodies and select judges who all flock to Holiday Inn By the Bay for this annual warm-up. Ticket prices for unlimited samples support Altrusa's literacy goals in Maine, so attendees can feed minds while feeding themselves.

Holiday Inn By the Bay
88 Spring St.
207-797-4494
altrusaportlandgivesbooks.org/chili-chowder-challenge.html

GET FREE ICE CREAM
AT SUSAN'S FISH-n-CHIPS

Greater Portland families descend on Susan's Fish-n-Chips four times a year when Susan's motivates area school children with free ice cream for good report cards.

Cards must be the most recent semester up to grade six, and they need to have them reviewed by staff. Kids delight as employees heap accolades on students' accomplishments—some students seem to enjoy that more than the ice cream! There is no purchase needed for children to be awarded their cup or cone; however, the restaurant offers an obvious solution for dinner while collecting your student's tasty reward.

Formerly a Morrills Corner auto repair shop on a busy road, Susan Eklund's family-run restaurant is not what most expect when imagining a quaint seafood shack in Maine. Looks are deceiving though. Once inside, the decor is decked with ship wheels, lobster traps, and fishing nets, and the back patio outside makes diners forget they're not at the shore. Live lobsters troll their tanks and fish fresh off the boat are on the menu. Reasonably priced with alternative choices for carnivores and vegetarians, it's a local favorite no matter the GPA.

1135 Forest Ave.
207-878-3240
susansfishnchips.com

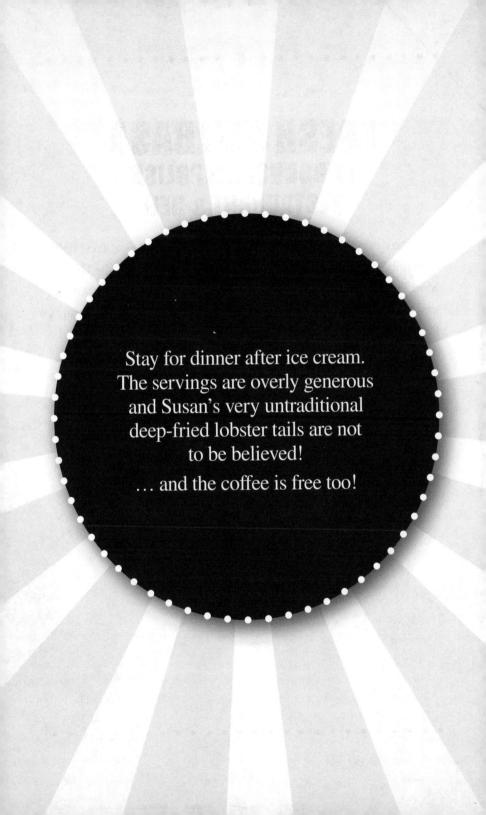

Stay for dinner after ice cream.
The servings are overly generous
and Susan's very untraditional
deep-fried lobster tails are not
to be believed!
… and the coffee is free too!

FRESH KIELBASA
AT BOGUSHA'S POLISH
RESTAURANT & DELI

Bogusha's is not a fake or a fluke—it's authentic Polish food done right. Bogumila Pawliczyk started out of the small storefront on the edge of Morrills Corner two decades ago, which makes the feeling that you've time-traveled back a century accurate. Originally from Poland (not the spring), Pawliczyk creates fresh food from family recipes, including casing the central European sausage on-site.

Not smoked or cooked, Bogusha's kiełbasa is an old-world holdover that is not easily found—or appreciated—in the U.S.

If cooking isn't on the agenda, the staff (all Polish) will prepare the sausage, along with several other specialties, authentically. With few tables and tighter quarters, enjoying the Polish-food breath of a dining companion is imperative.

825 Stevens Ave.
207-878-9618

THAI CHILI SAUSAGE
ON THE THIRSTY PIG'S BACK DECK

On a pleasant day, kick back with a beer on the back deck of the Thirsty Pig. Overlooking the castle-like grandeur of the former armory is reason enough to be there. Pair that beer with the Thai chili sausage sandwich and the experience is complete.

The Exchange Street eatery is a surprise, specializing in a variety of pork sausage offerings—and an impressive lineup it is. The Thai chili stands out as a flavorful selection that has enough spiciness to enhance the taste without overpowering or searing the palette. If you catch it right, a skilled beer-sommelier-like bartender will know the perfect pint to pair. Choosing which beer will best complement the specific flavors of each sausage is truly an art form.

37 Exchange St.
207-773-2469
thirstypigportland.com

NOTE: There are a couple of menu items to stave off a vegetarian-veto vote if dining with friends.

VINTAGE WINE
ON A VINTAGE VESSEL

Sommelier Erica Archer leads wine wannabes on an educational Wine Wise tasting tour aboard the *Frances*, a 74' gaff-top cutter. With cushioned benches and sides higher than most sailing schooners, the guests are less likely to find themselves overboard due to wind, sea, or wine.

"Wine is about exploring and being adventurous," Archer says of the nautical tastings. "I purposefully try to not have the same wine twice so the tastings are as unpredictable as the weather. However, we won't sail in bad weather and we won't drink bad wine!"

The two-hour voyage from Maine State Pier also educates about Portland, sea life, and sailing history for interested passengers, even allowing honorary deckhands the chance to hoist a sail or pilot the ship.

Frances's owner, Megan Jones, expertly sails her, allowing connoisseurs to comfortably tack through Casco Bay's islands within toasting distance of three prominent lighthouses. Even dedicated teetotallers may join their friends in the fun.

Departs at Maine Sailing Adventures at Maine State Pier
207-619-4630
winewiseevents.com

Archer pairs each voyage as she would a meal. "There's usually a huge selection of cheeses, but we sometimes have oysters or a chef aboard as well."

No matter what the theme is, "I pick wines that are unexpected—off the beaten path and fun. I typically do four really good wines and save a spectacular one for last." Archer intimates, "It's fun to have people's eyes get wide on that last tasting and go, 'Wow!'"

For connoisseurs without sea legs, Archer offers year-round wine (and food) walking tours on land in town.

EAT LIKE A LOCAL
AT HARVEST ON THE HARBOR

"Harvest on the Harbor is nothing less than a food euphoria," WLOB radio host Ray Richardson tells listeners when describing Maine's multiday food festival. "I'm a big guy, and I know food! There is nothing like this anywhere else in the world."

Set in breathtaking locations around the Portland waterfront in fall, high-end events take place at Ocean Gateway Pier. At the annual Grand Tasting, over three hundred people soak in harbor panoramas and sample beer, wine, spirits, and fine cuisine from as many as forty top culinary offerings around the state. The 5,590-square-foot Ocean View Room also hosts the Maine Lobster Chef of the Year competition, a selective juried tasting of the state's most creative *Homarus Americanus* preparation. To qualify, chefs are nominated, selected, and in some cases advance as culinary winners from other lobster festival contests in Maine. The winner receives state bragging rights and gets to present on the Maine stage at the Boston Wine Expo.

For a comprehensive Maine food experience, foodies attend the Marketplace session on Saturday. Always presented in a large venue, the popularity outgrew itself in the first year, forcing the Greater Portland Convention + Visitors Bureau to break the day into two halves to comfortably accommodate well over two thousand foodies.

14 Ocean Gateway Pier
207-772-4994
harvestontheharbor.com

OTHER MAJOR FOOD FESTIVALS

Maine Brewers Festival

Maine Vegetarian & Vegan
Food Festival

Taste of the Nation

ALL-YOU-CAN-EAT FISH & CHIPS
AT THE PORTHOLE

"To the Porthole!" exclaims Old Orchard Beach–native Michael Ruoss. "It's our battle cry." Ruoss, now a New Orleans chef, enjoys the popular waterfront restaurant and pub perched on Custom House Wharf whenever he's home. If it happens to be a Friday, then the all-you-can-eat fish & chips is on the menu! Taking a page out of the Roman Catholic playbook, the restaurant's nod to traditional values also makes marketing sense in a town so awash in seafood eateries. The Shipyard Beer–battered fish is served with french fries and cole slaw. The first serving is generally overly generous. If a customer is really hungry—just coming back from a week at sea or hasn't eaten all day—a second order might be in order. If a third is needed . . . well, who cares? It's all-you-can-eat!

The Porthole opened in 1929, and has managed to retain its authentic working-waterfront charm for over eighty-five years. Media tries to capture its Maine mystique, as the Porthole pops up in car commercials and Tommy Hilfiger fashion catalogs. The interior has been called "harbor-chic," with uneven floors, a long counter, and views of the wharf. An expansive deck offers highboy seating as well as picnic benches. A blind seal the staff calls "Sylvester" frequents the water below, instinctively knowing where the food is. But while looking for him, a seagull may drop in and stare you down for the leftovers!

20 Custom House Wharf
207-773-4653
portholemaine.com

MAINE LOBSTER ROLL
AT JOE'S SMOKE SHOP & SUPER VARIETY STORE

Portland is known for lobster, and more than that, lobster rolls. Joe's Variety is known for . . . not food. Most locals don't even venture in far enough past the adult magazines to discover one of the best food counters in the city hidden in the back. Yet this unassuming (some would say sketchy looking) store at Longfellow Square serves one of the best and most affordable lobster rolls in Portland.

Typically served through the summer, like a true Maine creation Joe's serves them the way lobster rolls should be: a generous portion of lobster meat, lettuce, a dollop of mayonnaise, all on a toasted hot dog roll.

Delicious, but still get it to go.

665 Congress St.
207-773-3656

TANDOORI CHICKEN
AT MR. BAGEL (DOWNTOWN)

All Mr. Bagels in Maine are not created equal. As a franchise, the locations wisely are allowed to tweak their menu to appeal to their location, location, location. Rash Sandhu's downtown location embraces its cosmopolitan customers—as well as Sandhu's culture—to infuse menu items unique to this bagel shop, including his signature tandoori panini.

Originally from Punjab and educated in England, Sandhu keeps the surrounding art college students and office workers walking extra blocks for dishes other Mr. Bagels don't have. Ignore any heavy sighs or eye rolls with the extra work that goes into creating the panini—the smell alone will ease feeling a little guilty for inconveniencing the overwhelmed staff during lunch rush. The first bite will completely eliminate any guilt.

"I am not a foodie—no way," Sandhu says. "I like experimenting, and being able to add a little of my own culture is fun."

Spicy both in flavor and heat, it's moderate enough to not dissuade those with milder taste, but enough to keep fans of Punjabi cuisine eating more.

539 Congress St.
207-774-8582

LOBSTER GARLIC SMASHED POTATOES
AT DIAMOND'S EDGE

By the time you realize the lawn overlooking the dock on Great Diamond Island is shaped like a martini glass, it's clear that Diamond Cove (aka Cocktail Cove) will be the ideal spot for a Diamond's Edge aperitif. On the grounds of former Fort McKinley, Diamond's Edge Restaurant & Marina is accessible by Casco Bay Lines ferry or private craft. Nestled in the island's quiet side, the patio and indoor tables gaze out to the boats sailing Hussey Sound's nautical highway and Long Island across the channel.

The scenic summer spot's real draw, however, is the food with a view—particularly the lobster garlic smashed potatoes. The menu is understandably seafood heavy, but also features eclectic American fare including southern fried chicken, a BBQ pork sandwich, and a grilled chicken wrap. But all the items seem incomplete without Diamond's Edge's signature side dish. Artfully prepared with Maine's famous crustacean, it's a perfect Portland complement to any entrée or sandwich. Ordering it alone isn't a bad idea either.

One Diamond Ave.
Great Diamond Island
207-766-5850
diamondsedgerestaurantandmarina.com

TAP THE KEGS
AT THE SHIPYARD BREWERY

While dozens of breweries have sprouted up around the city over the past decade, many winning prestigious awards, Shipyard Brewing Company's factory looms in the East End as a living monument of the neighborhood's working-class roots. The brewery is open for beer lovers to take free tours, roam the extensive gift shop, and taste the numerous brands made on the premises. Shipyard's line of Captain Eli's flavored root beers allows the tour and tastings to be a family experience.

When Shipyard opened in 1994, there were few craft beers being made. But Portland's rising tide in culinary arts has raised some other ships, or rather, glasses—and the city has developed into something of a beer town, recognized by *USA Today* as one of the "Top 10 Beer Towns" in 2014.

86 Newbury St.
207-761-0807
shipyard.com

TIP: Although the Shipyard Brewery doesn't have dining on the premises, you can eat at their restaurants: the Inn on Peaks (Peaks Island), the Sea Dog Microbrewery (South Portland, Topsham) and Federal Jacks (Kennebunk).

OTHER PORTLAND BREWERIES & BEER TOURS INCLUDE

Allagash Brewing Co.
207-878-5385
allagash.com

Bunker Brewing Co.
207-450-5014
bunkerbrewingco.com

Foundation Brewing Co.
207-370-8187
foundationbrew.com

Geary's Brewing Co.
207-878-2337
gearybrewing.com

Peak Organic Brewing Co.
877-212-1186
peakbrewing.com

Rising Tide Brewing Company, LLC
207-370-2337
risingtidebrewing.com

The Maine Brew Bus
207-200-9111
themainebrewbus.com

EAT, JUST BECAUSE,
AT FORE STREET RESTAURANT

Just *eat* at Fore Street. That's it. *Anything.*

It really doesn't matter what it is because it will be excellent. And if one does catch an off night (never heard of one, but we'll go with the possibility), Chef Sam Hayward and his staff will ensure it is corrected. Wait staff have been known to suggest visitors from Manhattan select another dish rather than relaying an order for a "very well-done, no pink," prime rib. They ate the prime rib as prepared, loving every bite.

Portland's explosion on the food scene may be recent, but one of the original fuses was the converted industrial brick restaurant on its Old Port namesake street. It isn't a waterfront eatery, it doesn't have great views, and there is no deck to escape the loud, dimly lit dining room, but the food is exceptional.

Since opening in the summer of 1996, Fore Street has been continually recognized by *Gourmet Magazine* and the James Beard Foundation, including Sam Hayward's award as Outstanding Chef, Northeast. Topping culinary lists internationally, the restaurant also impresses with a knowledgeable and efficient wait staff that ensures the presentation equals the cuisine.

288 Fore St.
207-775-2717
forestreet.biz

If you are able to sneak in, a leather chair in the front bar
and a reservation (well in advance!) in the quieter side
of the dining room are both worth the wait.

GARLIC CHICKEN PIE
AT PIZZA VILLA

"It's our signature pie—everybody loves it," says Jo Martin of Pizza Villa's best-selling garlic chicken creation. "It's always been there."

The ten-inch pizza starts with white-meat chicken chunks sautéed in garlic and olive oil. The meat is mixed with chopped spinach and feta cheese and baked to consistent perfection in minutes. The flavors hit the roof of the mouth before the first bite is even taken, and then let the eating begin.

If traditionalists are not ready to go so garlic all at once, "you can get half of the pie chicken and garlic, and the other half cheese and pepperoni," Martin reassures. "People can't decide, so we do it all the time."

When asked why his sought-after pizza only comes in ten-inch pies, owner Phil Regis always laughs, "I got a good deal on the pans in the '60s."

940 Congress St.
207-774-1777

EGGS BENEDICT
AT HOT SUPPA'

"I would be a vegetarian, but can't do it as long as Hot Suppa' makes eggs Benedict," says regular Steff Deschenes. "Canadian bacon, barbecue pulled pork . . . oh my God, the fried green tomato! Yeah, not going to happen."

The pint-sized eatery just outside Longfellow Square is a West End favorite and usually sees lines out the door for any meal. Brothers Moses and Alec Sabina wanted to present a solid representation of American classics inspired by their culinary exploration largely south of the Mason-Dixon line. Spicy and flavorful, the poached eggs over an English muffin with hollandaise sauce and choice of meat (or tomatoes) are served with fresh fruit and Geechie Boy grits or hash browns.

703 Congress St.
207-871-5005
hotsuppa.com

TIARAS & TONIC
AT VENA'S FIZZ HOUSE

This popular downtown spot hosts Portland Ballet's nod to the *Victorian Nutcracker* (set in the historic Victoria Mansion) one day during the Christmas season. With ballet students demonstrating moves in the shop windows, guests sip *Nutcracker* mocktails (alcohol-free cocktails).

"We just have fun with the whole *Nutcracker* theme—drinks for each dance of the show, but the Sugar Plum Fairy is the most popular," says owner Johanna Corman. "It was made with chai syrup, plum bitters, and a special sugar."

The dance company's prima ballerinas are also on hand to meet fans as the live window vignettes draw thirsty patrons into the mixology bar. "We really want to make ballet more accessible to people," Corman explained. Successful for both Vena's and Portland Ballet, the organizations look forward to building on the tradition, possibly introducing new events together throughout the year.

The popular Old Port establishment is noted as one of the top spots in Portland and has attracted the likes of Julia Louis-Dreyfus and TV food guru Alton Brown. "I've never seen anything like Vena's before," Brown says on his blog. "I suggest ordering a Lumberjack Love."

345 Fore St.
207-747-4901
venasfizzhouse.com

WINE IN A BLIZZARD
AT MJ'S WINE BAR

"Welcome to life inside the snow globe," says MJ's owner Mark Ohlson as guests stomp off the accumulating snow in the downtown bar. Its expansive walls of glass open to views of swirling flakes throughout City Center into Lobsterman Park and Canal Plaza beyond.

MJ's Wine Bar (and let's be clear here—wine *only*!), named after Ohlson's mother, Mary Jane, is a large space with a welcoming U-shaped bar, back tables, and a lounge area with plush leather couches defying you to leave. If the piano's ivories are being tickled or a jazz trio performs—baby, it's cold outside!—it may take a dogsled rescue to actually get someone to leave.

"While I have lived in the beautiful wine regions of France, Spain, New Zealand, and California, [Portland] is still my home," Ohlson shares in his online love letter. And he clearly likes having people over.

If a snowstorm hits Portland the third Thursday in November, MJ's Beaujolais Nouveau Day party will be even more legen—wait for it—dary!

One City Center
207-772-1400
onecitywines.com

A great spot in all seasons, MJ's Wine Bar has a large patio for summertime sips outside and features a year-round waffle brunch on Sundays.

REAL ITALIANS
AT AMATO'S

Not all sandwiches are created equal, nor should they be. There's little point in getting a cheese steak hoagie outside the Philadelphia city limits, po'boys belong in New Orleans, New York is for heroes, and grinders are Boston, but Italians are all Portland.

Like the other sandwiches, there is a story behind the name, and it starts with Giovanni Amato in 1902. An Italian immigrant (made the connection yet?), Amato started selling rolls stuffed with meat and veggies to Portland's waterfront workers from a cart. His first store on India Street still thrives and the business has more than forty shops in the northeast.

Amato's lists "Amato's Original" Italian consisting of "ham, American cheese, onion, pickle, tomato, green pepper, olive, salt, and pepper and oil." Their most popular sandwich, some swap the core ingredients for a more Italian combination of Genoa salami, capicola, prosciutto, and provolone. Non-traditionalists opt for turkey, roast beef, pepperoni, tuna salad, chicken salad, or—say it ain't so, Giovanni!—veggie Italians.

Regardless of an affinity for another region's sandwich love affair, Amato's sandwich is definitively Portland and it needs to be tried.

Original shop: 71 India St.
207-773-1682
amatos.com

ICE BAR
AT THE PORTLAND HARBOR HOTEL

Just as the last of the holiday hangovers subside, Portland Harbor Hotel keeps the bubbly flowing at their annual Ice Bar in January. The luxury hotel takes full advantage of its outdoor courtyard, which is all but avoided in the winter months, by constructing a massive network of carved ice that would make Disney's Queen Elsa proud.

The event spans a weekend in late January when the temperature typically doesn't melt the furniture. Often sold-out weeks in advance, it's a highlight for the winter-loving Mainers who enjoy the colder months almost more than the warmer ones. Gouges in the frozen surface create ice luges, cooling ingredients as they pour down the bar, swirling together as the alcohols meet in a drilled funnel, pouring perfect martinis in a glass below. Outdoor beer bars keep options open while a fully-stocked indoor bar has cure-alls for cold-related numbness . . . possibly creating a different kind of numbness.

468 Fore St.
888-798-9090
portlandharborhotel.com

NOTE: Portland Harbor Hotel offers discounts on rooms for patrons who may need to be put on ice afterwards.

LFK BURGER
IN LONGFELLOW SQUARE

There is no way to describe how much this is *not* "just another burger." On the paper menu, it reads pretty basic, but the unexpected explosion of flavor makes this one of the top burgers you may ever eat.

Topped with pimento cheese, bacon, and garlic mayo on a buttery dark pretzel roll, LFK's handmade juicy burger is memorable. Unless you request otherwise, it's automatically prepared a perfect medium-rare and served with bacon-sprinkled potato salad that has a hint of vinaigrette.

LFK is unique. Fashioned as a writer's bar, Longfellow's influence is impossible to ignore. The Longfellow Square location even has Longo's statue looming outside an oversize plate glass window. Inspiration is in the woodwork—literally—as bar rails are supported by typewriter keys spelling out Emily Dickinson's poem *After great pain, a formal feeling comes.* Vintage Woodstock and Smith Corona typewriters sit in cubbies. Blank paper waits at the ready above the antiques for any aspiring Hemingways eager to start their novel before their burger is finished. It's the kind of place that actually finds one wishing for Longfellow's famous lament—"The day is cold, and dark, and dreary"—as an excuse to stay longer and order again.

188A State St.
207-899-3277
facebook.com/LFKportland

BE A SCOFFLAW
AT BRAMHALL PUB

Approaching the daylight basement entrance to the Victorian townhouse is a bit intimidating. Descending the stairs, the former speakeasy begins to feel more like *Cheers*. Entering Bramhall Pub, numerous candles glow among intimate tables and booths, instantly conveying a relaxed, easy comfort.

The Bramhall was originally envisioned as a wine cellar for the elegant brownstone fronting the Congress Street's Parkside neighborhood. Intricate brickwork, arches, and an open (candlelit) fireplace make it easy to imagine the racks full of vintage labels.

A longtime local hangout, the former speakeasy was recently reinvented by former customer Mike Fraser, returning the venue to its roots as a secret subterranean gin joint—there's not even a sign outside. In keeping with this theme, "the Scofflaw is a Prohibition-era cocktail," offers waitress Kristen Nadasdi. Made with rye whiskey, cocchi Americano, lemon, and house-made grenadine, she's convinced "this is never going away." Not surprisingly, eater.com tapped Bramhall for having Maine's Bartender of the Year within weeks of its opening.

Live music and inventive pub fare is on the changing menu, but because Fraser is determined to keep it a neighborhood bar, prices are surprisingly moderate.

769 Congress St.
207-805-1978

PIEDMONTESE BEEF
AT PORTLAND REGENCY HOTEL & SPA

Regardless if the craving is for a filet mignon, New York sirloin, tenderloin carpaccio, taco salad, or just a burger, this Old Port luxe hotel (reimagined in the city's former armory) has three very different dining experiences to pair with their superior Piedmontese beef. From the hotel's private farm, the meat is "known for its high protein content while being lower in fat and cholesterol than turkey." And it's delicious.

Twenty Milk Street's wood-panelled ceiling evokes the quiet pre-hipster elegance of the Oak Room, with a brick fireplace and a cozy table in the front turret. "I keep trying Fore Street [restaurant], but I just like it here more," says Portland Symphony Orchestra flautist Alison Hale at her pre-concert haunt. "Really, it's just my favorite place!"

Live music is often in all venues. While the entertainment varies, it's frequently (and appropriately) jazz standards.

20 Milk St.
207-774-4200
theregency.com

OUTSIDE: The Garden Café spreads through a grassy oasis amid the Old Port bustle. A wooden privacy fence and gas-fired torches complete the outdoor illusion of tranquility next to a busy unseen parking lot.

DOWNSTAIRS: A secluded U-shaped bar tends to patrons in the Armory. The cocktail lounge is enhanced with faux bookshelves and the ambient glow of candlelight.

DARK CHOCOLATE SEA SALT DOUGHNUT
AT THE HOLY DONUT

"The dark chocolate sea salt outsells anything else we have," says Exchange St. clerk Allison Fisher of the Holy Donut. "We can't keep enough around."

The Holy Donut was a taste sensation in Portland before the doors ever opened. Excitement was driven by Leigh Kellis's take on the traditional doughnut that is definitively Portland—made with mashed Maine potatoes.

Instantly celebrated by national media, the original Parkside shop began rolling out innovative flavors, but the dark chocolate and sea salt flew off the racks faster than Kellis could make them—literally.

Offering something for everyone, many doughnuts are gluten-free. Egg-free, cinnamon sugared, and fresh berry glazed vegan doughnuts don't compromise on flavor. Don't be fooled by the primary ingredient—the Holy Donut's pastries defy density and are flaky. The complement of sea salt combined with the dark chocolate is a balance that hits all the mouth's sensations perfectly.

Whether the choice is the original Parkside shop or the Old Port location, get there early. They won't last.

194 Park Ave.
207-874-7774

Seven Exchange St.
207-775-7776
theholydonut.com

OTHER FLAVORS

Vanilla, maple, pomegranate, lemon,
Maine's own Allen's Coffee Brandy,
and the mojito made
with fresh mint

On the other end of the spectrum, a
bacon/cheddar-filled choice (with no
actual hole) is another wildly
popular selection.

BANANA-PECAN PANCAKE
AT BINTLIFF'S AMERICAN CAFÉ

Banana haters are not out in the cold on this bucket-list breakfast—it won't convert them, but it will wow. Served as a three-stack, double-stack, or even just as a single, the buttermilk specialty has Maine blueberry and chocolate and/or peanut butter chip options, but don't be swayed from this nutty-fruit flapjack. If perfection is the goal, add veggie homefries with thick-cut applewood smoked bacon, Canadian bacon, maple breakfast sausage, or andouille sausage. And for goodness sake, don't cheap out—pay for the Maine maple syrup.

This Bayside restaurant is a Sunday brunch institution with lines out the door in any season, in any weather. Owner Joe Catoggio keeps his frame building seeming more like a meal at a relative's home than an impersonal dining experience. Large windows allow light to flood into the dining areas, and images and memorabilia decorate the walls. The open kitchen serves from the ground floor while the upstairs bar works around the pitched roof. Summer keeps the wait time down with extra tables on an upstairs deck off the back.

Only open for breakfast and lunch weekdays, skip the line and get a reservation on weekdays. Life is too short.

98 Portland St.
207-774-0005
bintliffscafe.com

FRENCH FRIES
AT DUCKFAT

This gourmet sandwich shop opened in the East End in 2005, intent on making sure the unappealing name explains it all. Believed to be among the healthiest of animal fats for cooking, the flavorful base is the reason eyeballs roll in ecstasy to the back of diners' heads. Of all the offerings, Duckfat's Belgian fries consistently evoke that emotion.

Nancy Pugh and Rob Evans know the appeal of their side dish, often ordered as a nonshared entrée, and don't pull punches about it. They flatly state, "Hand-cut Maine potatoes, fried Belgian-style in duck fat, tossed with our seasoning salt and served . . . with your choice of eight homemade dipping sauces—these fries are our inspiration and the reason we opened Duckfat." Sauces include garlic mayo, lemon-herb mayo, truffle ketchup, horseradish mayo, Thai-chili mayo, and toasted curry mayo with a nominal additional fee.

Unpretentious, the restaurant does not take reservations, and tight quarters make for long lines at peak hours. Some might ask if it's worth the wait, but the answer is with the regulars at the back of the line.

43 Middle St.
207-774-8080
duckfat.com

MAINE FOODIE TOURS
THROUGH DOWNTOWN

The challenge in a foodie destination like Portland is twofold: how to sample all the great food and how not to put on the pounds doing it. Pam Laskey introduced her simultaneous solution to Portland in 2008 with Maine Foodie Tours. The two-and-a-half-hour stroll stops at more than a half-dozen notable shops and restaurants, allowing guilt-free tastings of several offerings at each location.

Partnering with some of the most delectable eateries downtown, the culinary tours mostly amble through Portland's wharves and Old Port while sampling locally sourced lobster, crab, fish, wines, and confections. The tours are led by guides who explain the city's farm-to-table movement as well as it's storied history. Surprisingly, they are all interlocked in unimagined ways.

Beyond the original Culinary Walking Tours, Laskey's tours offer something for all tastes including the Food Sherpa Tour, the Lunchtime Lobster Crawl, and one for happy hours (a two-hour tour). Most will leave you stuffed, others just full enough to keep going. Maine Foodie Tours are also available in Kennebunkport, Bar Harbor, and Rockland. Well-behaved canine companions may enjoy a specialized tail-wagging tour.

Start locations differ.
207-233-7485
mainefoodietours.com

TOUR DE FORCE

Other niche tours also uncover aspects of Portland.
Some combine forces and may offer referral or
online discounts, including:

The Maine Brew Bus
37 Exchange St.
207-200-9111
themainebrewbus.com

Summer Feet Cycling
233 Commercial St.
866-857-9544
summerfeet.net

Wicked Walking Tours
Bell Buoy Park
207-730-0490
wickedwalkingtours.com

BREAKFAST
AT MARCY'S

Marcy's Diner has been hiding in plain sight amid Arts District storefronts since 1989. A throwback to your grandparents' morning spot, it's wildly popular with the creative economy hipsters and Maine College of Art students nearby. Decked out with Americana memorabilia and vintage signs, the diner is as irreverent as it is delicious—the site's web address says it all.

Marcy's opens early for breakfast and closes after the lunch crowd dissipates. Lunches are good, but breakfast is the reason to go. The tiny downtown diner takes no reservations and only accepts cash. Expect to be one of the few patrons to not be greeted by name. Wait staff are not unpleasant as much as crazy busy, so take no offense if a smile is not immediately available—and don't plan on ordering with the conditional indecisiveness of *When Harry Met Sally* . . . it won't end well.

47 Oak St.
207-774-9713
nicemuffin.com

OTHER LOCAL BREAKFAST FAVES

BreaLu Café
428 Forest Ave.
207-772-9202

Hot Suppa'
703 Congress St.
207-871-5005
hotsuppa.com

Miss Portland Diner
40 Marginal Way
207-210-6673
missportlanddiner.com

The Porthole Restaurant & Pub
20 Custom House Wharf
207-773-4653
portholemaine.com

Ruski's Restaurant & Pub
212 Danforth St.
207-774-7604

OKTOBERFEST
AT NOVARE RES

Tucked behind the bustling shops of Middle and Exchange Streets is Novare Res Bier Café—an oasis for beer lovers to hide while loved ones shop. The stone and brick interior is dimly lit even on the brightest of days and practically screams "Welgekomen!" as you enter.

Latin for "to start a revolution," Novare Res owners Eric and Julie Michaud pledge "a beer drinking revolution . . . [striving] to serve what we feel are the best beers legally available to us in the state of Maine combined with the determination to try to support the small craft movement all over the world."

Despite protests of "*not* trying to be a German bier garten," the outdoor patio and selection of expertly crafted draught brews from the fatherland make little difference come Oktoberfest. The bar honors the feast by pouring limited styles of bier in one-liter "maas" based on Munich's celebration (typically the last weekend in September or first weekend in October).

Dorstig yet?

4 Canal Plaza
207-761-2437
novareresbiercafe.com

MUSIC AND ENTERTAINMENT

SHAKESPEARE IN THE PARK
BY FENIX THEATRE COMPANY

Friends, Portlanders, countrymen, lend them your ears! Fenix Theatre Company will make you laugh, cry, and cheer as they present the plays—both comedic and tragic—of William Shakespeare in the natural beauty of Deering Oaks Park.

For those who find the Bard dry, these free performances that bring his characters to life are more than worth the cost of admission. The troupe's energy and talent engage audiences emotionally as well as physically. Taking the famous "All the world's a stage" line to a new level, cast members pop up throughout the Olmsted-designed park, interacting with the audience.

A relaxing way to spend a weekend evening, shows run Thursday, Friday, and Saturday evenings in July and August. Performances are free, but donations to keep them open to all are appreciated.

Deering Oaks Park Ravine
207-400-6223
fenixtheatre.com

There are no seats, so bring a blanket or folding chair.
Many audience members bring a picnic to the play.
Also remember gobs of Deet for the mosquitoes.

JAY YORK CONCERTS
IN BAYSIDE

Entering the 1916 grange-style church on the downhill slope leading to Portland's Back Cove, you suddenly realize two things: the eclectic musical lineups are anything but ecclesiastical, and you're actually in someone's living room. Jay York's Last Church on the Left is literally that, at the bottom of the one-block street in the shadow of Maine's tallest building.

York bought the former church from the Moonies in 1990 and creatively adapted the structure to serve as his in-house photography studio and home. His inspiration of opening his living-room nave to stage live concerts began as a fund-raiser for St. Lawrence Arts. Now, performances number around eight a year. Notification is by word of mouth or e-mail only. Acts come from around the world, but all donations received go "100 percent to the performer," says York.

As a low-income and blue-collar industrial part of downtown, Bayside is going through a gentrification that is both welcomed and vilified by polarized segments of the community. York's contribution to Portland's performing arts skillfully walks a tightrope by feeding the aspirations of the creative economy while maintaining enough of a bohemian low-profile approach to not ruffle neighborhood feathers.

58 Wilmont St.
207-773-3434
facebook.com/events/618054454951884

STUMBLE ALONG
WHARF STREET

"Dining out on the cobbles, beneath flickering, period gas lamps is an agreeable faux-time travel experience," says *USA Today* of Wharf Street's romantic nineteenth-century atmosphere, naming it one of the top ten Prettiest Cobblestone Streets Across America. Lined with shops, restaurants, nightclubs, and cocktail lounges, people are often seen losing their footing on the uneven pavers whether it be due to the high heels or highballs.

Closed to vehicles during evenings, all ages are represented when walking the thoroughfare. Steep steps and sidewalks bring people down from the rest of the Old Port to enjoy two blocks filled with everything from French cuisine to Giant Jenga. The street is conveniently bookended by the historic Mariners Church building—with art galleries, a billiards club, and a pub—on one end and the Portland Harbor Hotel on the other.

Out for a night on the town, a romantic stroll, or just to people watch, Wharf Street has something for everyone. Just ask anyone at the Bar of Chocolate.

Runs from Moulton Place to Union St.,
between Commercial and Fore Sts.

THE EVER-CHANGING LIST OF WHARF STREET BUSINESSES

Beals Old Fashioned Ice Cream
Portmanteau
Port Boutique
Gritty McDuff's Brew Pub
Amigo's Mexican
Joseph's Men's Clothing
Central Provisions Restaurant
Street & Co. Restaurant
Bonfire
Bar of Chocolate
Rogue's Gallery Clothing
Ollo Hair Salon
Oasis Night Club
51 Wharf
Buck's Naked BBQ
The Merry Table—French Restaurant and Crêperie
Pearl

'80s NIGHT
AT BUBBA'S SULKY LOUNGE

Paying the cover charge at the door of Bubba's famous (and sulky) retro dance party every Friday night is a toll into Bayside's *Twilight Zone*. A Portland institution for close to fifty years, '80s Night is a relatively recent invention catering to those from the Brat Pack era, appropriate since Judd Nelson is a Portland native.

But the dance music from bands—some wildly popular and some even still touring—transcends *The Breakfast Club* crowd. '80s Night is timeless—or is it ageless? The disco-era dance floors (holdovers, even by Bubba's standards, from 1977's *Saturday Night Fever)* find octogenarians dirty dancing with millennials. Much of the under-thirty crowd are authentic in drop-shoulder sweatshirts, teased hair, and side ponytails.

But Bubba's is the real star here. The low-rise lounge is deceptively large inside. The venue seems shockingly endless—there are rooms, and side rooms, and sub rooms. Two island bars bookend the building, the one fronting Portland Street evoking a bus station lounge, the one in the back providing a lively dance oasis available for private parties. The vintage lunch boxes hanging from the ceiling are worth the cover alone, but then the other memorabilia takes focus. It's what Cracker Barrel might have looked like had it started in Maine.

92 Portland St.
207-828-0549
bubbassulkylounge.com

How *anyone* born before 1969 is not here *every* Friday night is hard to comprehend.

Reasonable cover charges await and it's cash only, so budget appropriately or bring your ATM card for the rogue cash machine. 90s Night is Saturday!

SUNSET CONCERTS
ON THE WESTERN PROMENADE

The sun setting over the White Mountains stretching into New Hampshire has a soundtrack when viewed from the edge of Bramhall Hill on Tuesdays during the summer. A free concert series is scheduled at various city parks for weeknights in July and August, and the Western Promenade enjoys variations on folk music while the last rays disappear over Mount Washington more than seventy-five miles away.

The Western Promenade is lined with stately stone and brick mansions from the robber-baron days. The homes were built to claim enviable sight lines west. As the city expanded over the centuries, the undulating horizon's foreground was marred with Portland International Jetport and the state's largest retail mall with surrounding shopping centers. It all makes a beautiful and ironic backdrop to the music born of a counter-culture society. You almost expect Joni Mitchell to get out when a big yellow taxi pulls up.

There is something relaxing and a tad bit dizzying about the spectrum's swirl of colors splashing in the sky. It intensifies when an acoustical guitar accompanies soothing vocals in perfect harmony. Or maybe that's just the smell in the air.

Western Promenade
207-874-8826
portlandmaine.gov

OTHER FREE CONCERTS

Wednesdays
Kids' Concerts
12:30 p.m., Deering Oaks Park

Thursdays
Jazz Concerts
7 p.m., Fort Allen Park

Live at Five
Rock Concerts
5 p.m., Monument Square

JULY FOURTH
ON THE EASTERN PROMENADE

On the morning of the Fourth of July, blankets and chairs are set out on the Eastern Promenade's expansive bluff as soon as the sun rises in anticipation of the Stars and Stripes Spectacular more than twelve hours away. Food trucks, vendors, and police roll up to serve the masses. By evening, Munjoy Hill closes to nonresident cars, clearing the streets for pedestrians. Scores of boats moor in earshot of the annual concert. A respectful hush quiets seventy thousand excited patriots when the Portland Symphony Orchestra takes the stage.

After soul-stirring tributes to America, starting with the national anthem, the conductor guides the audience through patriotic music both relevant and historical. Then, as the final embers of daylight fade, maestro Robert Moody raises goose bumps with the opening notes of Pyotr Ilyich Tchaikovsky's *1812 Overture.*

Just when kids are bored by the fifteen-minute classical piece, the tempo changes, signaling its famous crescendo. It climaxes with pyrotechnics in place of the composer's cannon fire. As the music concludes, a full fireworks show begins. Funded by generous sponsors when city hall failed to fund the celebration, the explosions over the harbor impress with dramatic scale and duration.

Eastern Promenade
july4thportland.org

Portland's hillside makes for perfect stadium seating, but if enjoying the crowded hillside isn't your thing, VIP seating with table service is available for a premium.

Wherever you sit—no matter how early you go—remember the concert and fireworks end *after* dark and the car is most likely a mile or more (unlit) walk away. Bring a head lamp or flashlight to navigate the uneven terrain.

MAGIC OF CHRISTMAS
AT PORTLAND SYMPHONY ORCHESTRA

When conductor Robert Moody emerges from the wings of Merrill Auditorium in his red Santa hat, the tone is set for Portland Symphony Orchestra's traditional holiday concert series, which runs for two weeks in December.

"Magic of Christmas is one of the longest-running performances by a professional orchestra in the country," says Moody. "The PSO has been performing it for [over] thirty-five years."

As the baton turns to strike up the orchestra, every musician is donning antlers, flashing hats, red reindeer noses, elf ears, or another nod to the season. The jingling bells elicit a cheer as the PSO takes the audience on its annual *Sleigh Ride*, complete with simulated cracking whip.

While truly a concert celebrating the wonder of the Christian holiday, Moody does an excellent job of not alienating those of other faiths by accentuating and educating. In expounding on the magic of the season, he also presents the significance of the music and the traditions created and shared throughout Western cultures. Moody expertly explains the relevance of Christmas to classical composers and contemporary pop culture in an inclusive manner without condescension, honoring the significance of the holiday for the faithful and the children in attendance.

20 Myrtle St.
207-842-0800
porttix.com

Try not singing during the Christmas Carol sing-a-long.
I double-dog dare you.

SEE BOB MARLEY . . .
EVERYWHERE

First of all: No, not the late reggae star. *This* Bob Marley is a Portland-based stand-up comic. He often personally mans his kiosk at the Maine Mall. A local celebrity who thoroughly enjoys his loyal following, Marley has appeared in films and TV, most memorably as an over-zealous policeman and comedic foil to Willem Dafoe's hyperfocused detective in *The Boondock Saints* films.

His humor is so localized that the punch lines almost seem like inside jokes for locals in the audience—and sometimes they are, making the confusion of flatlanders in the crowd part of the fun. But his rants on parents, family, and trying to get downtime "Upta Camp" (translation: Mainers heading up north to vacation homes, which are referred to as camps) are universal themes—once you get past the Maine accent and colloquialisms—to which everyone relates.

Bob Marley is not a hard man to find. His comedy CDs and DVDs are numerous. He is a spokesman for various local businesses on TV, and he is seemingly always performing somewhere. He performs at small clubs regionally and does concerts for area nonprofits and schools as fund-raisers, yet his holiday performance series through New Year's still consistently sells out Merrill Auditorium. People cannot seem to get enough of him. No wonder he needs to go upta camp.

bmarley.com

DANCE IN THE STREETS
AT THE OLD PORT FESTIVAL

Like nowhere else, the Old Port Festival welcomes the warm weather to Portland's downtown the first weekend in June. The waterfront district is alive with multiple stages—rock, country, folk, and more—and food vendors catering to musical and culinary tastes of all kinds. A single-day event for more than forty years, the festival has expanded into a weekend event that includes June's First Friday Art Walk, working waterfront tours, city discovery competitions, and a ninety-foot Ferris wheel with commanding views of the city and harbor.

Live performances sprinkled around the city blocks and parks include dancing, juggling, comedy, and cirque-styled aerial acrobatics by students from the Circus Conservatory of America. Rock climbing walls, bounce houses, face painting, and other children's activities ensure that everyone is smiling.

The festival performances and concerts are all free, but vendors and rides often have fees.

The Old Port Exchange District
207-772-6828
oldportfestival.net

ROCK AND ROLL ALL NIGHT
AT THE STATE THEATRE

Many major cities have a classic Art Deco–style theater, but the State Theatre's classic motif is accented with Moorish decor, making it feel more like *Casablanca* than Portland. Inside the venue's performance space, 1,680 fans have enjoyed, screamed, danced, and rocked from the sweeping balcony to the mosh pit. A standing bar in the right orchestra section keeps the liquor flowing without missing a beat.

Beginning as a movie theater in 1929, the State Theater was originally designed to have a "capacity of 2,300," relates general manager Lauren Wayne. "It operated as a first-run movie house until the late 1960s, when it became a porn theater."

After decades of fits and starts, the State finally found steady footing under Wayne's leadership with a New York City promotion and management company. With additional support from Live Nation concerts, the venue has catapulted the Arts District hot spot to new heights.

The theater has hosted great names in music. The eclectic collection of window cards includes Elvis Costello, Pat Benatar, My Morning Jacket, George Thorogood, Arctic Monkeys, Lyle Lovett, and John Hiatt.

609 Congress St.
207-956-6000
statetheatreportland.com

BE SACRED & PROFANE
AT BATTERY STEELE

On the Saturday after the harvest moon, graffiti artists, tightrope walkers, jugglers, performance artists, and admirers of all things counterculture find their way to the hidden halls of Battery Steele. Celebrating the change of seasons through the arts, commercialism is shunned in the Sacred & Profane Festival.

Overgrown with grass, shrubs, and natural fauna throughout the concrete fortification, Battery Steele isn't so much hidden as it is inconspicuous. The 1942-constructed World War II fortification stands sentry on Peaks Island's eastern foreside. Brilliant depictions by some of the world's foremost street artists mix with those of locals on the vast man-made cave walls. Sculptures, installations, and performances add to the merriment as lights attempt to illuminate the "profane" creativity amid the "sacred" walls of the battery.

In keeping with the event's motif, the annual festival is not advertised or promoted. Either it's known, or it's not. Word of mouth reminds those who may not be following its pagan-based timetable.

21 Central Ave. Ext.
Peaks Island

Formally known as "U.S. Army Corps of Engineers Battery Construction #102," it is thought to be the "largest battery ever built anywhere in the United States," according to the book *An Island at War* by Kim MacIsaac and historian Joel Eastman.
A grand canvas for the repressed emotions—good and bad.

NOONDAY CONCERT
AT FIRST PARISH CHURCH

Jazz and classical music wafts from Maine's oldest continually operating church Thursdays from March through mid-April. The Portland Conservatory of Music performs free concerts for a lunch break crowd in the Unitarian Universalist's granite First Parish Church.

Founded in 1995, the Portland Conservatory of Music trains musicians of all ages for professional careers or simple love of music. First Parish serves as a wonderful performance space with the lovely acoustics expected in a traditional meetinghouse. The concerts offer a unique opportunity for students to perform for an audience hungry for a springtime interlude—and lunch.

With its congregational roots going back to 1632, the current 1826 church replaced its wooden 1740 predecessor known as Old Jerusalem, which was located in the same spot. Retaining the previous steeple tower, clock, bell, and Drowne weather vane, the transition between the houses of worship also discovered a cannon ball from the 1775 British destruction of the city (Old Jerusalem had not otherwise been damaged), now incorporated in a chain suspending the church's glass chandelier. Maximize the experience by enjoying the school's musical interlude from the Longfellow pews 1 and 2, where Henry Wadsworth Longfellow's extended family attended services.

425 Congress St.
207-773-5747
firstparishportland.org

HEAR A SILENT MOVIE
WITH THE KOTZSCHMAR ORGAN

Seeing a black and white silent movie filling Merrill Auditorium's massive old-school silver screen creates an overwhelming sense of nostalgia. When the music emanates from the pipes of the Kotzschmar Organ, the reverberations make the age before "talkies" a tangible reality.

Portland's premier performance space turns itself over to Hollywood's two-dimensional art form, but the real star of the show is the massive 6,862-pipe organ, the second largest in the world when installed in 1912. It was named after Hermann Kotzschmar, the incomparable organist at First Parish Church when the instrument was gifted to the city by *Saturday Evening Post* publisher Cyrus H. K. Curtis (whose middle initials represented the close family friend for whom he had been named).

Friends of the Kotzschmar Organ shows several famous films from the silent era in Merrill Auditorium, but the Halloween screenings are the most fun, particularly Lon Chaney's over-the-top and completely appropriate *Phantom of the Opera* (1925). When the silent movie is married with the Kotzschmar's sound, it's tempting to scan the balconies for the masked figure with his sweeping cape.

20 Myrtle St.
207-553-4363
foko.org

ALL THAT JAZZ
AT PORT CITY BLUE

Blue is a little nightclub in the Arts District with all the trappings of a Greenwich Village venue . . . without the high prices and crazy crowds. Shoehorned between a cluster of bohemian shops and restaurants, the melancholy music is pure Portland. The narrow bar serves wine and beer accompanied by a small plates menu for folks as they squeeze in at long tables. The name is deceiving in that no one genre is represented. Samuel James will appear for some guitar riffs evoking an atmospheric Delta blues. He can be followed by Rob Sylvain's foot-stomping Acadian Aces, whose energetic French-Canadian tunes are so deeply ingrained into Maine's heritage. Or there's even Shanna Underwood's country showcase. There are long-standing lineups like Wednesday night's nod to Irish music, but the weekends belong to jazz. Saturday nights feature three acts, 6 p.m. until midnight. On Sunday afternoons, a jazz jam invites anyone on stage to join the band—but they need to bring their own instrument or voice. The song book runs the gamut from classics to contemporary.

650A Congress St.
207-774-4111
portcityblue.com

WALK CONGRESS ST.
ON FIRST FRIDAY ART WALK

It's one thing to walk along Congress Street sneaking peeks at new art work and dodging in and out of gallery openings (pass the wine and cheese, please) every first Friday of the month. It's quite another to *take over* Congress Street. Portland's Downtown District teams up with Creative Portland to turn the city's major downtown thoroughfare into the state's largest pedestrian mall for select Art Walks during the year.

The traffic-free stroll is anchored on Congress Square in the shadow of the Portland Museum of Art (open and free), spanning the city's spine up to the public library at Monument Square. Beyond free admission to artists' receptions, open studio tours, and several art museums, the entire boulevard becomes a stage with entertaining street performers, musicians, acrobats, fashion shows, theater scenes, dancers, and an occasional flash mob mixing in with the roving audience.

First Friday Art Walks are rain, shine, or snow, year-round.

Congress Street from Congress Square to Monument Square
207-370-4784
liveworkportland.org/arts/walk

SPORTS AND RECREATION

CARRIAGE RIDE
THROUGH THE OLD PORT

After the city's fifty-foot holiday tree is lit, horses pull carriage rides through the Old Port every half hour on weekends between Thanksgiving and Christmas. Children are excited to experience a piece of rural nostalgia in Maine's largest urban setting, and holiday shoppers are happy to sit for a while as they ride along the city streets soaking in the holiday spirit.

Starting in Monument Square, the horses lead holiday revelers into the Old Port, down by Exchange Street's shops, past Fore Street clubs, and return through the financial district, with a final turn at First Parish Church before gathering more passengers at the base of Portland's 1891 Soldiers and Sailors Monument.

These free trips down Portland's memory lane are a tradition sponsored by Portland's Downtown District. The organization's goal of enhancing the downtown experience for holiday shoppers has inspired several events designed to lure people away from suburban shopping, even for a little while, and to remind them of the joys of silver bells in the city.

Monument Square
207-772-6828
portlandmaine.com

CATCH A LOBSTER
ON LUCKY CATCH CRUISES

Experience the ins and outs of catching your own lobster dinner on Lucky Catch Cruises. The ninety-minute voyage launches from Long Wharf and is led by experienced lobster man Captain Tom Martin. *Lucky Catch* passengers are excited to don bright orange protective gear in order to bait and haul traps, with an option to buy (at boat price) any acceptable-sized lobsters they catch—a business model believed to have been created by Tom Sawyer while whitewashing a fence.

Captain Tom presents a brief but informative lesson on industry rules and regulations with emphasis on which catch is legal to keep.

Launched in 2007, the forty-foot lobster boat has been modified to comfortably accommodate passengers where stacks of traps would normally be stored. Those along for the ride can absorb the lessons of lobstering while taking in the picturesque Calendar Island's lighthouses and historic harbor forts. Many tours even encounter seals frolicking around the boat while seagulls circle with hungry anticipation.

170 Commercial St.
207-761-0941
luckycatch.com

When back in port, take your catch to Portland Lobster Company at the end of the wharf. They will cook it to your liking for a nominal charge so you can catch your lobster and eat it, too!

DELIVER THE MAIL
WITH CASCO BAY LINES

Legend has it that Captain John Smith explored Casco Bay before he met Pocahontas. Overwhelmed by the number of islands in the protected harbor, he communicated to the king of England that "there were as many islands in the harbor as days of the year." So the Calendar Islands were named. Some attribute this to Colonel Wolfgang William Römer, but either way, in reality the U.S. Coast Guard charts only 221 islands, some barely big enough to stand on at high tide. Several large Casco Bay island communities are within the Portland city limits.

"The ten o'clock boat's been doing that run year-round since the 1890s," boasts Larry Legere, the ferry service's unofficial historian, making it the "longest-operating freight service of its kind in the country." You can do the three-hour delivery cruise around Casco Bay and visit half a dozen islands, stopping long enough for a quick hop on the docks for a photo op. Get a glimpse of the summer cottages. If it's early enough in the day, passengers can get off one boat and explore an island before catching the next one. It's often hours between deliveries, so be prepared to relax. A water taxi can rescue those who get stranded (or bored).

If longer visits are required, Portland's Casco Bay Lines ferry service to the islands scattered about the harbor is a great way to get out on the water inexpensively no matter the weather!

56 Commercial St.
207-774-7871
cascobaylines.com

ISLANDS SERVED BY CASCO BAY LINES FERRIES

Bailey Island
Town of Harpswell

Cliff Island
City of Portland

Great Chebeague Island
Town of Chebeague Island

Great Diamond Island
City of Portland

Little Diamond Island
City of Portland

Long Island
Town of Long Island

Peaks Island
City of Portland

LIVE A FIELD OF DREAMS
AT HADLOCK FIELD

On the final Sunday game of the season, a hush comes over the sold-out crowd when a disembodied voice announces, "If you build it, they will come." A tingle of delight slides up the back of the neck as Portland Sea Dogs baseball players in vintage uniforms slowly emerge from the corn stalks in center field. Then, they come into the stands and shake everyone's hand!

This AA farm team for the Boston Red Sox is a fun, family-affordable chance to see professional players on their way to the majors—most of the 2004, 2006, and 2012 championship Red Sox teams' players paid their dues on Hadlock Field. Also the home field for Portland High, it's even a field of dreams for Portland-area high schools, whose homegrown talent gave Major League Baseball infielder Ryan Flaherty and pitching ace Charlie Furbush.

271 Park Ave.
207-879-9520
seadogs.com

If baseball isn't your sport, Portland is also home to several other professional teams:

Portland Pirates
(Arizona Coyotes AHL hockey)
Cross Insurance Arena
94 Free Street
207-PIRATES
portlandpirates.com

Maine Red Claws
(Boston Celtics D-League basketball)
Portland Exposition Building
239 Park Ave.
207-210-6655
nba.com/dleague/maine/

The Port Authorities
(WFTDA Maine Roller Derby team)
Calamity Janes
(WFTDA Maine Roller Derby B-team)
The R.I.P. Tides
(WFTDA Maine Roller Derby C-team)
Portland Exposition Building
239 Park Ave.
mainerollerderby.com

Portland Boxing Club
Portland Exposition Building
239 Park Ave.
207-761-0975
portlandboxingclub.org

TURKEY BOWL GAME
AT FITZPATRICK STADIUM

For over a century, the battle between Portland's two oldest public high schools captures Maine's attention at their 10 a.m. kickoff on Thanksgiving Day. Not limited to alumni, up to 6,300 fans stream into Fitzpatrick Stadium to build up an appetite—or escape relatives—and see if the Portland High Bulldogs or Deering High Rams football team will capture bragging rights for the next year.

It began as a friendly rivalry in 1874 when Portland's only high school—the second-oldest in the country—played border city Deering's new high school team. The rivalry intensified after the city of Portland annexed Deering in 1898, effectively making the two high schools crosstown rivals.

"It almost divides the city a bit on Thanksgiving morning," former Deering football team captain (and current Baltimore Orioles infielder) Ryan Flaherty told ESPN in 2008. "People are intense."

The Thanksgiving game began in 1911, and has evolved into an annual tradition. With the high school football season officially over days earlier, the event is little more than an exhibition game with high stakes.

Portland holds the all-time win record, but Deering has a commanding lead so far in the twenty-first century. Pass the gravy, please.

Fitzpatrick Stadium
100 Deering Ave.
207-756-8275
portlandschools.org

Aside from
one cancellation in
1920 on account of bad weather,
the Portland-Deering game has
withstood rain, wind, and shine better than
the postal service.

An amusing legend surrounds the 1971
Thanksgiving snowstorm, according to ESPN's
Rachel Lenzi in a 2008 commentary. She relates
that Portland school officials tried to call off
the game. Attempting to phone, it became
clear the storm had knocked down the
lines and they couldn't get through.
. . . Game on!

PLAY BILLIARDS
IN THE PORTLAND CLUB

Walking into the second-floor billiards room at the Portland Club, it's hard not to automatically scan the room for Jackie Gleason's Minnesota Fats sipping his White Tavern whiskey before mechanically clearing the table in front of an incredulous Paul Newman. The expansive room is famed architect John Calvin Stevens's shrine to billiards.

Previously the home of the Hunnewell-Shepley family, the State Street mansion was designed by Alexander Parris in 1805. After purchasing the building in 1922, the Portland Club added a ballroom and commissioned Stevens to modify Parris's arcade. The portico parapet was removed, Palladian windows and caps were added, and the original columns were replaced.

There are twelve antique mahogany tables—six pool and six billiard—on the second floor mixed in among the others. Popular for celebrations, gatherings, and contests, the room captures the affluence and elegance of the pre-Depression era.

156 State St.
207-761-6665
theportlandclub.org

RACE A BOAT
AT MS HARBORFEST

In mid-August, when the summer sun and harbor water is at its warmest, Casco Bay hosts three days of nautical arm flexing. MS Harborfest's seafaring competitions are designed to excite boaters and landlubbing spectators alike, while raising money to combat multiple sclerosis.

Starting with a welcoming reception and fund-raising auction on Friday, the skippers also meet for a friendly reception (and to size up their competitors). White triangles fill the blue seascape surrounding Portland on Saturday as the sailing regatta dominates the day. But Sunday is all about power!

Sunday's quiet is shattered when high-powered engines of lobster boats and tugboats roar at the mouth of the Fore River. Smaller crafts create a waterway drag strip for lobster boats to cut through the harbor for bragging rights.

The tugboat muster finds the workhorses gathering from around the state for a noble nod of mutual respect in a procession in the harbor before attempting to outgun each other in speed races and nose-to-nose pushing duels.

Experiencing this diverse waterfront community join together to raise money to combat Multiple Sclerosis, a degenerative neurological disease, is reason enough to be here.

eventmam.nationalmssociety.org/harborfest

ICE SKATE
IN DEERING OAKS PARK

When the wind blows cold, the skates come out! Portland is one of the great remaining cities that embraces ice skating in its city park. The picturesque pond, fronted by an adorable 1894 Frederick Thompson stone castle, was once connected to the tidal basin of Portland's Back Cove. The pond has provided free skating to residents for more than a couple of centuries, and figure skaters and hockey players still hit the ice at all hours.

The setting is so magical that a romantic skating scene was filmed with Denzel Washington playing an angel who falls for Whitney Houston in *The Preacher's Wife* (1996). Envisioned by the Olmsted Company, it's not surprising that Deering Oaks and its pond—reminiscent of the landscape design company's other park projects in New York City—served as a stand-in for the Big Apple setting.

Deering Oaks Park pond
207-756-8275
deeringoaks.org

Bring your skates, as there are none to rent.
Also, check the castle hours with the city if you
want to warm up . . . or use its indoor bathrooms when you go.

DECK THE HULLS
IN THE PARADE OF LIGHTS

Hang the lights, illuminate the decorations, blast the music, and start the engines for the annual Parade of Lights in Portland Harbor. Festively lit vessels of all classes, shapes, and sizes join a procession looping around Portland Harbor every second Saturday in December.

Tugboats lead sailboats, yachts, small power boats, and Casco Bay Line ferries in a circle from the harbor island to the Casco Bay Bridge. Tugboat captains become nautical ballerinas, spinning the massive boats while maintaining course and speed during the procession. Fireworks shoot off a waterfront pier to the delight of shoreline spectators, signaling the finale.

If you don't have your own boat, hop aboard Casco Bay Line Ferries. One ship has a full bar on board, the other does not . . . but *that* vessel is BYOB!

Ticket sales benefit the Sail Maine program. This nonprofit helps underprivileged children in this seaport city learn how to harness the power of wind and experience the joys of sailing.

56 Commercial St.
207-774-7871
cascobaylines.com

SKI THE STREETS
OF PORTLAND

Noted by *USA Today* as one of the top urban cities for cross-country skiing in the United States, it is not uncommon to see locals gliding down Exchange Street, enjoying a full-body cardio commute after a snowy nor'easter.

A few inches of powder over Old Port cobblestones creates scenic city byways for Nordic urbanites happy to hit the snow from their door. But even if the snowplows restore traffic before you're ready to return, Portland Trails's interconnected web of paths runs parallel with city streets and waterfront vistas, offering visual distractions on the way home.

Anywhere in Portland

IF THE STREETS ARE PLOWED, OTHER POPULAR SPOTS INCLUDE:

All of Portland Trails • Eastern Promenade • Western Promenade • Evergreen Cemetery • Deering Oaks Park • Payson Park • Baxter Woods • Mackworth Island • Riverside Golf Course

If you want the workout but prefer walking, snowshoeing is a popular alternative.

FINISH
THE MAINE MARATHON

"People who don't run the Maine Marathon are missing something fun . . . especially when the knees go out at mile sixteen," laughs runner Laura Peterson. "I didn't care if I crawled—I was crossing that finish line."

The sense of accomplishment is only part of the drive to run early October's twenty-six-mile race—it also traverses some of the loveliest byways in the region. Starting with a deceptively easy two miles around the western side of Portland's Back Cove, the course heads north on Route 1 across Casco Bay into Falmouth. Runners bear right up Route 88, beginning the hills on this Foreside Road through Cumberland. The journey continues to the turnaround at Yarmouth's Prince's Point.

The return retraces the hills along the leafy mansion-lined road back to Portland. Energy from the community bolsters runners, with residents cheering the competitors in the suburban towns. Back in Portland, runners pick up the Back Cove trail again through Payson Park for the home stretch. The finish in Portland is "family friendly," Peterson says. "Our kids are able to come out at the end and run across the finish line with us." Props are given to first-time marathoners as finishing times are announced to the crowd.

Start at Baxter Blvd. near Preble St.
207-749-9160
mainemarathon.com

CELEBRITY WATCH
IN THE OLD PORT

Portland's world-class recording studio, scenic locales, burgeoning culinary reputation, and homegrown talent seem to be attracting more celebrities to the city. Sit back and enjoy the show.

Billy Joel, Eric Clapton, and many recording artists are frequently found at the waterfront while in town recording with Bob Ludwig at Gateway Mastering or simply getting away.

Leonardo DiCaprio has been spotted dodging recognition at the Portland Harbor Hotel, and a pregnant Julia Roberts famously lived at what is now the Westin Portland Harborview while her husband filmed a movie. The Westin's guests also got to see Ray Wise, Michael Cassidy, and Maria Thayer trying to save the world from zombies on the hotel roof.

Kirsten Dunst has dined at Fore Street. Rob Morrow sang for his supper at the Porthole. Alton Brown tweeted his love of Vena's Fizz House with the world, and Adam Richman, Anthony Bourdain, Eric Ripert, and various TV food show celebrities keep returning to this culinary destination.

It's not unusual to spot Anna Kendrick, Liv Tyler, Glenn Close, Judd Nelson, Linda Lavin, Andrea Martin, Christopher Fitzgerald, Victoria Rowell, "Survivor Bob" Crowley, and Robert Plant in town while visiting relatives over holidays and vacations.

Anywhere in the Old Port, with emphasis on Tommy's Park, Long Wharf, Exchange Street, and area restaurants.

GOOD CELEBRITY-SPOTTING SPOTS

The key to celebrity sighting in Portland is to ignore them and be completely unimpressed.
It's the Maine way, ayuh.

Long Wharf
Tommy's Park
Post Office Park
Fore Street Restaurant
Portland Harbor Hotel
Portland Regency
Exchange Street

BASKETBALL FINALS
AT THE CROSS INSURANCE ARENA

It's not March Madness, but it's close! In the last week in February, state basketball championship games are played in Portland. It may not be the collegiate rivalries facing off the following month, but you'd never know it by the deafening chants coming from the Spring Street arena when the two top high school teams in their class reach the hardwood.

One of Portland's high schools often makes the cut. If a hometown team takes the floor, you may need earplugs. If two face off, earplugs won't help. When Deering High School (est. 1874) won its first state championship in 2012, it may as well have been the NBA finals at Boston Garden.

You don't need to like basketball to enjoy the enthusiasm and passion of the crowd at a championship game, but it's wise to not wear one team's colors on the other team's side of the arena—even accidentally!

45 Spring St.
207-775-3458
crossarenaportland.com

CHEER LIKE A LOCAL (and wear the colors)
Portland Bulldogs (Class A): blue & white, bark a lot •
Deering Rams (Class A): purple & white • Cheverus Stags (Class A):
purple & gold • Catherine McAuley Lady Lions (Class A, all-girls):
green & gold • Waynflete Flyers (Class C): green & white

RAPPEL A HIGH-RISE
FOR RIPPLEFFECT

"It's terrifying and a hell of a lot of fun," says Shannon Bryan about her experience descending from one of the tallest buildings in Portland. "As scary as it is, take five seconds to look around . . . just don't look down."

The 180-foot drop in Monument Square, normally associated with rural cliffs, is open to one hundred folks looking for an urban adventure. The opportunity to abseil is afforded to those who secure $1,000 or more in fund-raising for Rippleffect, a nonprofit supporting youth development and leadership, largely through kayak-related programs. The one-day event in mid-May supports Rippleffect's scholarship, education, and leadership efforts.

The event's safety is ensured with Over the Edge's supervision, a rappelling-event company with skilled professionals and state-of-the-art equipment to keep participants safe. With nothing below to break the fall, the equipment won't let you descend quickly, even if you want to. First-time rappellers can hone their skills beforehand on smaller buildings or parking garages nearby. Eyes closed the whole way down? A helmet cam will preserve the memory and even capture digital stills. Scream away.

One City Center
207-791-7870
rappelforripple.net

WHALE OF A TAIL
ON ODYSSEY WHALE WATCH

After seeing a whale breach for the first time, the drama and wonder of Herman Melville's *Moby Dick* takes on a whole new dimension. Odyssey Whale Watch tours depart Long Wharf from spring through late fall in search of the migrating undersea behemoths. While catching sight of humpbacks, finbacks, or minke whales is likely, it's not unheard of to also see sharks, North Atlantic white-sided dolphins, and sea turtles, as numerous species of seabirds escort the ship anticipating a free meal.

There are more tours in the warmer months when the daylight is longer, but the single-voyage months of spring and autumn are when whales migrate, so odds are better for multiple sightings along the way. The crew works closely with other marine professionals tracking the large mammals to set a course to meet them along their journey.

170 Commercial St.
207-775-0727
odysseywhalewatch.com

As warm as it may be on shore, it can be as much as ten to twenty degrees cooler on the open North Atlantic, so bring layers. If you're a flatlander or landlubber, or just prone to motion sickness, bring Dramamine . . . the trip over the ocean swells can be a four-hour roller coaster ride at times.

POLAR BEAR DIP & DASH
OFF EAST END BEACH

A collective shriek of shock and awe breaks the New Year's Eve quiet as a giant polar bear (okay, person in a polar bear costume) urges hundreds of people into frigid Atlantic waters at noon the last day of each year. It's the Natural Resources Council of Maine's annual fund-raiser, where people who are environmentally conscious, are checking off a bucket list, or have lost a bet, plunge into ocean water averaging thirty-seven degrees to bring awareness to global climate change and its effect on Maine.

Their dashing back onto the sand into warm towels held by friends, family, and supporters is not, however, the reason for the name. Those looking for a warm-up run beforehand can dash in a 5K race at 11 a.m. around the nearby Back Cove Trail. Shuttle buses deliver them to East End Beach for the noontime dip.

East End Beach is on the base of the Eastern Promenade and has the distinction of being the only beach in the city. The Munjoy Hill neighborhood location is convenient for attracting participants, and picturesque views of the Calendar Islands and harbor forts allow them to focus on anything else as they hit the water running. Chattering teeth can be used for eating at the celebration that follows in a local city pub.

No matter your scientific or political beliefs, a fun time is had by all . . . and the water's still *cold*!

East End Beach
nrcm.kintera.org/dipdash

CATCH YOUR BREATH
AT STANDPIPE PARK

It's hard to catch your breath at a place that takes your breath away, but do try and absorb the city panorama from this North Street park. Standpipe Park hides in plain sight. No one seems to know it by one name. It's called North Street Park, Fort Sumner Park after the World War II military installation on the site, Shailer Park after the adjacent former school building, or "oh, there!" This patch of grass owns one of the most picturesque precipices east of San Francisco's Pacific Heights.

From the ridge looking right, a glimpse of the blue harbor can be seen through downtown financial center high-rises pierced by the Cathedral of the Immaculate Conception's spires. Carrère and Hastings's distinctive city hall tower is almost blocked by Franklin Towers (Maine's tallest building). Further right, the Westin Portland Harborview seems almost the same height as Maine Medical Center's hilltop elevation. From there, the peninsula slopes down into the gentrifying Bayside neighborhood, where industrial brick warehouses and scrapyards are intermixed with coffee houses, breweries, and chain stores. Sleek towers suddenly pop up next to Back Cove's field of dazzling blue water. The oval outlined with emerald trees fades into the wavy horizon of the White Mountains to the west.

It's a calming portrait of Maine's largest city.

60 North St.

OTHER NOTABLE PUBLIC-SPACE VIEWS IN PORTLAND

Casco Bay Bridge
Seagull-eye views of the harbor and city will surprise.

Baxter Boulevard & Payson Park
Skyline across Back Cove

Western Promenade
Sunset over the New Hampshire mountains

Eastern Promenade
Over Portland Harbor looking "down bay"

IT MAKES A VILLAGE
ON MACKWORTH ISLAND

On the lee side of Mackworth Island is a clearing where natural elements from the surrounding woods create structures for the tiny fairies who inhabit the island. Inventive homes, stores, apartment complexes, and even an airport (fairies have to land somewhere) have popped up over the years. All the architectural acumen is useless without a good contractor, so children visiting the island construct the buildings with skillfully arranged twigs, leaves, branches, rocks, and whatever is found. Material foreign to the island is not allowed for ecological reasons.

Over the years the village has become more of a fairy city. It suffers from urban sprawl like so many popular areas impacted with overbuilding. But so many children know that if you build it, they will come, and everyone knows you can't have enough fairies around.

Island access off Route 1 at end of Andrews Ave.
Falmouth
trails.org/our-trails/mackworth-island-trail

Governor Percival P. Baxter deeded Calendar Island bordering Portland to create the Governor Baxter School for the Deaf. The deed required that the island always remain accessible to the public for recreation. Additionally, he included a provision ensuring that his pet cemetery with his beloved Irish setters and a horse also be preserved. Since then, the perimeter of the hundred-acre island is regularly trodden by thousands of people, many of whom come to house the fairies.

CIRCLE AROUND
BACK COVE

Most days, hundreds of urban dwellers (and four-legged companions) circle the tidal basin below the western slope of Portland's downtown. The Back Cove is surrounded by trails, paved roads, and athletic fields to unwind or enjoy nature. The three-and-a-half-mile loop is often used as a training course for 5K races and marathons, but it's also enjoyed for an easy stroll.

The body of water is a picturesque recreational backdrop for runners, power walkers, bicyclists, and—in winter—cross-country skiers. Anchored by two large parking lots at opposite ends, starting points can either be close to downtown in the shadow of the Intermed skyscraper or in the East Deering neighborhood's pastoral Payson Park.

Along the way, wildlife, flora and fauna, grand homes, and the city skyline are visually on hand to distract from "feeling the burn." Elegant double bridges were constructed in the early 1920s, and their now-consolidated waterside respite is still a picturesque half-way point. Rest or just take in the city.

If the route seems too short, Back Cove Trail connects into the seventy-mile labyrinth of Portland Trails.

trails.org/our-trails/back-cove-trail

CAMP OUT
AT FORT GORGES

Fort Gorges is a massive stone military fortress that seems to float in Portland's harbor. Its location is close enough for stunning views of the city skyline, but far enough to see a blanket of stars at night. Once in the hexagonal fort, its seclusion is enough to feel a world away from the nearby urban center . . . perfect for camping!

Built in 1857 and named after Ferdinand Gorges, an original landowner of Portland, the fort is a monument to nineteenth-century military architecture. Now listed on the National Register of Historic Places, the city-owned fort has no public transportation. A perilous approach by private craft requires skilled navigation. Beyond the arched levels, gunnery mounts, and torpedo storehouse, it's discovering the massive ten-inch Parrott gun settled in the grass parapet that excites visitors. Several people in length, the cannon was deemed too large to remove when the fort was decommissioned.

A well-used firepit is safely in the former parade grounds, but it is wise to bring wood as well as any other supplies. There are no trees in the fort, much less electricity, stores, or anything else. It's as close to roughing it as you can get in a city.

Hog Island Ledge in Portland Harbor
friendsoffortgorges.org

CONSPIRACY THEORISTS TAKE NOTE

Fort Gorges was constructed to defend Portland Harbor after the War of 1812. Dominating rocky Hog Island Ledge, it's strategically centered between Portland's Fort Ethan Allen (now a park), South Portland's Fort Preble, and House Island's Fort Scammell. Construction of the fort was authorized and begun under then–U.S. Secretary of War Jefferson Davis. By 1865, it was deemed obsolete during construction due to technological advances in weaponry during the Civil War and was never fully completed. Conspiracy theorists ask, what did the future president of the Confederacy know and when did he know it?

JEWELL FALLS
IN THE FORE RIVER SANCTUARY

In the heart of Portland, trails lead to a thirty-foot waterfall seemingly in the middle of nowhere. Accessible from some of the city's busiest thoroughfares, treks to the natural cataract meander at various distances in the eighty-five-acre Fore River Sanctuary, depending on the trail.

The picturesque stepped cascade of water is not as remote as it seems. In reality, Jewell Falls is only a stone's throw from residential homes in the Rosemont neighborhood. The falls are named after Tom Jewell, co-founder of Portland Trails, who also donated the land where the falls are located. While the isolated spot is enjoyable anytime of the year, the springtime Fore River runoff creates a mini Niagara Falls in the center of the city limits.

The most popular trailheads begin where Congress Street crosses the Fore River in Stroudwater (longest hike from the south) and Hillcrest Avenue off Brighton Avenue (closest hike from the north). Other starting points are at the end of Starbird Lane (east side) and Rowe Avenue (west edge), allowing access to the sanctuary trails from all sides. While other access is tempting, residential streets with convenient cul-de-sacs are often unwelcoming to the additional traffic.

Portland Trails
207-775-2411
trails.org

CULTURE AND HISTORY

DISCOVER YOUR MASK
AT THE MUSEUM OF AFRICAN CULTURE

Colorful, whimsical, disconcerting, humorous, and frightening are only a few descriptions for these masks—the oldest dating back to 1600 A.D.— in the Museum of African Culture's permanent collection. Largely comprising pieces from Africa's fifty-two sub-Saharan countries, the collection also contains bronzes, ivory flutes, and clay vessels dating back several millennia. Steeped with spirituality, the masks help tribes navigate life. This includes coming-of-age masks created from prophesies predicting young men's adulthood.

"African-born children progress through life and grow to become who they are to be. African children born in America are distracted in a culture of instant gratification influenced by what they see on TV," says museum founder and executive director Oscar Mokeme. "Buses come from Harlem and other communities bringing children—not just African American—to connect through our programs to try and realign their cultural values, kind of like adjusting their GPS."

An awe-inspiring example of quality over quantity, the small museum presents a rich history across a vast continent. National and international traveling shows supplement the past with relevant rotating contemporary art exhibits.

13 Brown St.
207-871-7188 or 207-899-6428
museumafricanculture.org

BE INSPIRED
AT WINSLOW HOMER'S STUDIO

People are often mesmerized seeing the sea-green waves churning foam as they dramatically crash on the rock-lined edge of Checkly Point. Such is the power of Winslow Homer's art. Many of his paintings in the Portland Museum of Art boldly depict Maine's coast. But Homer's work imitates life—his life—at his studio, now also part of the PMA, which offers guided tours.

A twenty-minute ride from the downtown museum, Homer's studio is in the exclusive enclave of Scarborough's Prouts Neck. After enjoying a decade of summers, the artist sought the peaceful beauty of Maine over Manhattan, hiring noted architect John Calvin Stevens in 1884 to convert a carriage house into a residence. His primary residence until his death in 1910, it's difficult to not feel the inspiration Homer drew from the natural surroundings outside his fifteen-hundred-square-foot studio.

Portland Museum of Art
7 Congress Square
(Studio tours are transported *only* via PMA's museum shuttle from downtown to 5 Winslow Homer Road, Scarborough.)
207-775-6148
portlandmuseum.org/homer

Prouts Neck is still a coastal retreat drawing celebrities. The journey out to the secluded area that Winslow Homer called home brings visitors past majestic homes of the rich and famous, including actress Glenn Close and NFL Commissioner Roger Goodell.

SEE THE LIGHT
ON MAINE OPEN LIGHTHOUSE DAY

Portland Harbor is protected by no less than five lighthouses, all within a ten-minute drive of each other (a private craft is required for the sixth). This cluster allows enthusiasts the opportunity to scale almost one-fifth of the state's towers during Maine Open Lighhouse Day. Organized by the Maine Office of Tourism and the American Lighthouse Foundation, cherished beacons normally off limits to the public are accessible during one Saturday each September.

While each of the sentinels in Casco Bay has a unique design and rich history, the one to not miss exploring is Portland Head Light. Commissioned by George Washington, the ninety-foot tower is a must-see. Classic in design and dramatic in setting, it is believed to be the most photographed in the world, sitting on majestic cliffs with crashing waves—right out of film noir.

Whichever you choose to visit, do not be discouraged by bad weather. Lighthouses were built to save ships in blinding seas, so experiencing a sweeping beam cutting through the rain on a stormy night may be the *best* way to see these beacons in action! And there is no better sound on a misty night than the low moan of a foghorn.

American Lighthouse Foundation
207-594-4174
lighthousefoundation.org

PORTLAND HARBOR LIGHTHOUSES (BY YEAR BUILT)

1. Portland Head Light, 1791, Cape Elizabeth
2. Two Lights/Cape Elizabeth Light—East, 1874, Cape Elizabeth
3. Two Lights/Cape Elizabeth Light—West, 1874, Cape Elizabeth
4. Portland Breakwater (Bug) Light, 1875, South Portland
5. Spring Point Ledge Light, 1897, South Portland
6. Ram Island Ledge Light, 1905, Ram Island

TIP

Portland Head Light, one of the most popular lights on Maine Lighthouse Day, has limited (free) tickets first come, first served, so go early! And you'll still have time for the others close by.

STAND ATOP
THE PORTLAND OBSERVATORY

Standing beside Portland Observatory's cupola, visitors are transported to a time before cell phones, walkie-talkies, and radio, when visual signals were the only way to communicate. Technological advances in navigation have rendered observatories obsolete. So much so that Portland's 1807 wood tower is the last of its kind on the entire continent.

During the age of sailing, shipment schedules were little more than a good guess. Ships would sail into port without warning and owners would scramble to find men to off-load the goods, which could take days. Captain Lemuel Moody had experienced this frustration firsthand, and was inspired by the ports of call with signal towers.

Moody constructed his tower at the apex of Munjoy Hill with a telescope capable of seeing a craft up to sixty miles away. Often taken for a lighthouse, Portland Observatory shares a similar design to withstand the same high winds and severe weather at its exposed position.

As visitors soak in the views of Casco Bay, the city skyline, and New Hampshire's White Mountains to the west, it's amazing to know signal towers like this were in far-flung ports, spotting incoming vessels to alert owners that their ship was literally coming in. Dock workers were assembled and waiting when the cargo arrived.

138 Congress St.
207-774-5561
portlandlandmarks.org/observatory

The Industrial Revolution was not the only threat over the years. Moody's tower was the lone wooden structure to survive the Great Fire of 1866. Tales were related of Moody's workers pouring water down the observatory's sides while the inferno was raging around them. It was the only standing structure in the East End neighborhood after the conflagration.

GET YOUR GREEK ON
AT THE GREEK FESTIVAL

You don't need a big, fat Greek wedding to be welcomed into a Greek family. Just head to the corner of Park and Pleasant Streets and shout "Opa!" one weekend in June. Laughter and dancing accompany the authentic music, food, and drink of the Mediterranean culture at the annual festival in Portland's West End.

"Any excuse to be Greek!" says Konstantina Rigas. The twenty-five-year-old enjoys embracing her heritage at Maine's largest Greek festival, coming thirty miles to dance and "express my Greekness—I'm all over it!"

Exuberant sounds and scents explode from a normally quiet Holy Trinity Greek Orthodox Church, inviting the world to celebrate. Flash mob Kalamatianós dances continue late into the night around stately Federal brick townhomes, as ouzo-happy revelers spontaneously break into the popular counterclockwise folk dance.

133 Pleasant St.
207-774-0281
holytrinityportland.org

Other Cultural Festivals: Festival of Nations, Italian Heritage Festival, Southern Maine Pride Parade and Festival

THE FIRE HORSES
AT PORTLAND FIRE MUSEUM

Nestled in the West End between State and Park Streets you can find a living tribute to the first responders throughout Portland's fire-prone past—particularly the Great Fire of 1866—in the Portland Fire Museum. This boutique museum is the retired Engine 4 station house that served downtown. Squeezed in among the antique trucks, wagons, memorials, and vintage equipment are the original horse stalls. While the original equine inhabitants of this house were full-time residents, the two current horses are here part time.

The city's great conflagration destroyed two-thirds of Portland's downtown on July 4 when firecrackers sparked off wood chips at the waterfront. The flames consumed most of the wooden structures in Portland, from the waterfront wharves all the way up trough the East End. It remained the worst urban fire until Chicago met Mrs. O'Leary's cow five years later.

The museum began in 1891 when the Portland Veteran Firemen's Association decided to share their memories of battling the blaze with generations to come. The PVFA has grown the collection over the past century.

Inside the granite firehouse, guests learn fire prevention. Explore the horse-driven water wagon, view vintage films featuring the museum when it was an active station, and visit the horses while soaking in the history.

157 Spring St.
207-772-2040
portlandfiremuseum.com

HALLOWEEN PARADE
THROUGH THE WEST END

Ghosts, princesses, goblins, sexy cats, giraffes, witches, superheroes, and politicians are but a few of the characters that join in on the fun of the West End Halloween Parade every October 31.

The neighborhood's parade starts in front of Reiche Community Center on Brackett Street at 6 p.m. and loops though the historic West End. A tradition for over thirty years, colorful fifteen-foot puppets lead masked marchers of all ages into the neighborhood's winding streets. Along the route, children jump out of the procession in their quest for candy.

The West End Historic District includes many Gothic homes that are listed on the National Register of Historic Places. These Victorian-style mansions enhance the haunted holiday's fun as trick-or-treaters bound up the steps of what could well be those of the Addams Family. One prominent resident even opens his carriage house for free haunted tours every year for all to enjoy.

While the nineteenth-century buildings hardly need decorations, many up the ante in a determined effort to preserve a tradition of door-to-door trick-or-treating in a welcoming community, creating joyful memories for another generation.

Reiche Community Center
166 Brackett St.
Oct. 31, 6 p.m.

COLONIAL LIFE
IN THE TATE HOUSE MUSEUM

The clapboard home in Stroudwater seems almost unremarkable compared to the large homes surrounding it, but the Tate House predates many of its neighbors by more than a century. The colonial-era home was constructed by Captain George Tate in 1755.

Founded in 1657, Stroudwater Village is situated along the Fore River as it widens into Portland's inner harbor. Captain Tate's home reflected his important role in the British Royal Navy, overseeing production of the ships' masts harvested from Maine's white pines—it's not called the Pine Tree State for nothing. From his prominent Georgian-style home, the captain could monitor progress as trees came downriver for shipment outside. With its subsumed dormer on a gambrel roof, extensive herb garden, and period furniture, the Tate House would have been considered enormous in the colonial era.

With the British Navy's destruction of Portland (then called Falmouth) in 1775, the Tate House Museum is one of the oldest remaining structures in Portland, and the only colonial-era residence open to the public. The eighteenth-century home is a National Historic Landmark.

1267 Westbrook St.
207-774-6177
tatehouse.org

HUNT BEARS
ON THE LANGLAIS ART TRAIL

At Ocean Gateway, visitors are greeted by an amusingly ferocious *Standing Bear* (1977) towering fifteen feet, while two *Playing Bears* (1976–77) sit by the grand staircase in Portland International Jetport. These are two examples of legacy artist Bernard Langlais.

Bernard "Blackie" Langlais's sculptures numbered in the thousands when he died in 1977. A small portion of his massive body of work is displayed throughout the city. His wood sculptures were gifted to Portland by Colby College and Kohler Foundation Inc. for display around the city as part of the state's Langlais Art Trail. His larger-than-life bear sculptures are hiding in plain sight, surprising visitors and locals alike.

langlaisarttrail.org

LANGLAIS ART TRAIL IN PORTLAND

Deering High School
Untitled, 1976–77, wood, paint, and nails; wood and paint,
36 × 20 × 17 in.; 37 × 16 × 15 in. Portland Public Art
Committee, gift of Colby College and Kohler Foundation Inc.
(two heads)

Portland High School
Untitled, 1977, wood and paint, 26.5 in.; 26.5 in.; 33.5 in.
Portland Public Art Committee, gift of Colby College and
Kohler Foundation Inc.
(three heads—the high school rivalry continues . . .)

University of New England Gallery of Art
Untitled, wood on wood, 64.5 × 29.25 × 3.5 in.
University of New England Art Gallery,
gift of Colby College and Kohler Foundation Inc.
(looks kind of like an abstract lobster)

Portland Museum of Art
Noon Exercise, ca. 1963, pine, 116 × 88.5 in. Portland Museum
of Art, purchased with support from the Robert R. Masterton
Memorial Fund and Helen Langlais.
(prancing horse)

Portland Public Library—Main Branch
Elephant, 1976–77, wood. Portland Public Art Committee,
gift of Colby College and Kohler Foundation Inc.

VISIT THE BERLIN WALL
ON LONG WHARF

People strolling along Long Wharf are often surprised to discover three panels of cement with faded graffiti from Germany that were once brightly colored depictions celebrating the Communist Party's fall from power in Europe. The most prominent of the whimsical images is of the Soviet hammer-and-sickle logo in flames boasting "The Party's Over!"

A reminder of the recent twenty-fifth anniversary of the eighty-seven-mile wall's destruction, the three panels are an unappreciated treasure on Portland's waterfront. Representing the oppression literally surrounding West Berlin for twenty-eight years, this section is one of only fifty-four in the United States.

Long Wharf near 170 Commercial Street

Also visit the Heroes Wall on Long Wharf and pay respect to the brave military from Maine whose contributions help secure the freedoms the nearby Berlin Wall fragments attempted to repress.

SEE, PRAY, LOVE
AT THE MAINE JEWISH MUSEUM

"Exhibits are by contemporary artists who must have a Jewish connection *and* a Maine connection," says Maine Jewish Museum curator Nancy Davidson. The museum is part of a still-active synagogue downtown. "Every two months we rotate shows." But the art isn't the only attraction. Stained glass windows in the simple brick edifice hint at architectural treasure inside. The sanctuary awes with "modest grandeur," boasting a domed ceiling and elegant woodwork familiar in houses of worship from the era.

Restored as an "unaffiliated synagogue—everyone is welcome!" explains Davidson. "The first floor is for shows and Orthodox services, and the sanctuary on the second floor is active and used for reform services." A third floor highlights original Jewish residents in Maine and their contributions. Occasional high-profile touring shows are also presented.

Formerly an apartment building, Etz Chaim ("Tree of Life") Synagogue was converted in 1921 by a congregation without a temple. The Tree of Life organization was formed and ensures Etz Chaim remains one of "the oldest European-style synagogues in continuous use in Maine."

267 Congress St.
207-773-2339
mainejewishmuseum.org

NEW YEAR'S EVE
AT THE VICTORIA MANSION

Traditional tuxedos and high-contrast dresses—some with white gloves—give life to the Victoria Mansion's Black & White Soiree. On the last night of the year, the formal fête welcomes midnight in a way Jay Gatsby would envy. Portland's Gaslight League hosts parties to complement the opulent Morse-Libby House (named after the two families that owned it) with over-the-top holiday cheer. The museum home, already decorated with period-appropriate extravagance for Christmas, is enlivened with the group's Roaring Twenties New Year's celebration.

"It's so opulent, you can't ever overdo it," says Dan Kennedy, owner of Harmon's & Barton's florist, who has contributed to the holiday decor since 1991. "I've developed a passion for decorating it."

The inspiration of development director Sam Heck, the self-described social club's membership consists of a "diverse and creative group of cocktail enthusiasts, partygoers, and history buffs."

The Gaslight League also parties with a hearty Mardi Gras Fête on Fat Tuesday (an obvious fit considering the New Orleans connection), a Steampunk Masquerade on Halloween, and a summer soiree.

109 Danforth St.
207-772-4841
victoriamansion.org

TIP

The home is open for public tours May-January, so the home, including Christmas decor, can be enjoyed regardless of Prohibition. Those who prefer a nightmare before Christmas can be enveloped in Victoria Mansion's Tales of Terror during Halloween. This, however, is no carnival haunted house. While creepy-looking folks may greet you, it is an evening of theatrical readings. If that doesn't sound frightening, then you've never heard Edgar Allan Poe done right. And, really, doesn't everyone dressed in Victorian-era clothing look like they could be Jack the Ripper?

• •

HISTORY

Ironically, the majestic brownstone was constructed for Ruggles Sylvester Morse as a summer home and would have never been inhabited during the winter holidays. The Portland native and New Orleans hotelier had the brownstone townhouse built (1858–1863) to escape the southern heat. Stuck below the Mason-Dixon line through the Civil War, he was unable to enjoy his new Italianate villa–style getaway for almost four years.

Joseph Ralph Libby bought the mansion, but made no significant alterations. Abandoned during the Great Depression, the landmark escaped demolition, and the museum was created in 1941. The Libby heirs donated furnishings the family had kept—over 90 percent—making the Victoria Mansion a veritable time capsule.

SUNRISE SERVICE
AT FORT ALLEN PARK

If sitting in a crowded church being hit by oversized bonnets isn't for you, join other faithful followers at Fort Allen's gazebo and be one of the first in the United States to welcome the Easter morning sun. The pre-dawn gathering is informal and casual. Fleece coats and L.L. Bean boots are more likely to be worn than silk dresses and high heels when people gather on the circular bandstand waiting for the sun.

All faiths are welcome to join. The Stevens Avenue Congregational Church doesn't discriminate . . . especially on Easter morning. As a United Church of Christ (UCC), the religious roots are deep in colonial New England Puritanism, but the modern-day church encourages interfaith celebration and inclusion. Strangers are welcomed as warmly as the congregation.

When the ocean begins to reflect the red streaks in the glowing sky, the people circle around to reflect on the day. Fort Allen's perch at the end of the Eastern Promenade hovers above the channel to the open bay, affording expansive views over Portland Harbor. The deep blue sky changes from red to orange, and then eases into a hot yellow as bright rays crest the Atlantic. The sun's climb over the ocean softens the brightening sky, sending sparkles across the waves below. Commuter ferries from Peaks Island glint in the morning sun as they pass by Fort Gorges.

Fort Allen Park Gazebo
207-797-4573

Easter dates differ every year, so the time of sunrise services changes. Services are rain or shine, because the assumption is that the sun is shining somewhere, so regardless, "He is risen, indeed."

RAINY DAY ROOM
AT WADSWORTH-LONGFELLOW HOUSE & GARDEN

Most people know the phrase, "Into each life some rain must fall" by Henry Wadsworth Longfellow, but few know where it was created. His 1841 poem *The Rainy Day* was composed in a room that overlooked the garden in the back of the family home. The desk on which he penned the poem still stands sentry. The Colonial Revival–style gardens in the back of the house are original, including an eighteenth-century lilac planting Henry may have cared for himself. It's open as a public respite amid the tall downtown buildings.

Some are under the misguided impression that literary giant Henry Wadsworth Longfellow is from Boston, but his childhood home fronts Congress Street in Portland's center city. Built by his grandfather, General Peleg Wadsworth, in 1786, the home remained in the family until Henry's sister, Anne, bequeathed it in 1901 as a museum, understanding her brother's profound impact on the world.

489 Congress Street
207-774-1822
mainehistory.org/house_overview.shtml

Henry's sister, Anne Longfellow Pierce, ensured the family estate remained as it was when her brother spent his childhood. She decided to preserve the home long before she passed away to honor his memory for future generations. This extended to never installing plumbing in the house. Throughout her life, until she died at age ninety-one in 1901, she resolutely crossed the street to city hall and renewed her privy license.

SING IN THE RAIN
AT THE UMBRELLA COVER MUSEUM

An exuberant accordion-wielding woman startles guests walking in this tiny Peaks Island museum, ready to pepper unsuspecting visitors about the wonders of the umbrella cover—that's right, no umbrellas, just the forgotten protective sheaths. If it looks uncomfortably like a room full of used prophylactics, she can show you the "X-rated umbrella cover room," which is (happily) a bit of an overstatement.

Founding director and curator Nancy 3. Hoffman (not a misprint— her middle name is legally "3") started her collection innocently enough. Discovering half a dozen umbrella covers, she didn't know what to do with them. A museum was born. Years ago, Guinness World Records recognized her cover inventory as the largest at 730, even though the covers now top 1,200. Would anyone else admit to having more? Hoffman hopes not! Her enthusiasm and energy is contagious.

"More people [find us], and every season gets better and better," she says. "The international press went bonkers."

Hoffman challenges visitors with jokes and contests that cannot be refused. But that doesn't hold a candle to her talent on the piano accordion. She seems to have a tune for everything and is ready to play at the drop of a hat. She sings songs in twenty-one languages (she only speaks four).

62-B Island Ave.
Peaks Island
207-939-0301
umbrellacovermuseum.org

THE MISSION STATEMENT SAYS IT ALL

"The Umbrella Cover Museum is dedicated to the appreciation of the mundane in everyday life. It is about finding wonder and beauty in the simplest of things, and about knowing that there is always a story behind the cover."

PAY YOUR RESPECTS
IN THE EASTERN CEMETERY

Portland's oldest public burying grounds is the Eastern Cemetery at the base of Munjoy Hill. As a colonial-era cemetery, it's on the National Register of Historic Places. With over thirty-five hundred recorded deceased, interments ceased during the Civil War.

The five-acre field has ornately carved headstones (and footstones). These memorials are impressive for their artistry as much as their history. A distinctive tombstone in the northwest corner with a carved soldier's bedroll marks the grave of Alonzo P. Stinson, who died fighting in the First Battle of Bull Run. He is the first Portlander known to be killed in the War between the States.

Other grave markers include two enemy ship captains, both mortally wounded in an epic sea battle during the War of 1812. British Captain Samuel Blythe surrendered the HMS *Boxer* to American Lieutenant William Ward Burrows II of the USS *Enterprise,* deciding the sea battle off the Maine coast before both masters died of their injuries. Ironically, they lie side by side forever in the rear of the graveyard.

224 Congress St.
spiritsalive.org

Eastern Cemetery is accessible even when locked. Visitors who want to pay respects when gates are closed only need cross the street to get the key from a local merchant—appropriately, vintage book dealer Carlson & Turner Antiquarian Books is the keeper of the keys. Otherwise, make arrangements with Spirits Alive, the volunteer organization that maintains the historic hallowed ground, keeping it open for the public.

241 Congress St.
207-773-4200
carlsonturnerbooks.com

OTHER PORTLAND CEMETERIES

Evergreen Cemetery, Deering Center
First Parish Church, Intown
Western Cemetery, West End

SEE A NATIONAL TREASURE
AT THE PORTLAND MASONIC TEMPLE

Few organizations have a deeper history or a lovelier building than the Modern Free and Accepted Masons. This international fraternal organization's membership reads like a history text. The grandeur of Portland's Masonic Temple represents the secret society's influence over the centuries. Home to Triangle Lodge No. 1 (the first lodge in Maine), it was chartered in 1769 and brought to Portland by Paul Revere. Not surprisingly, the temple is conveniently located across the street from city hall and next to First Parish Church—at the head of Temple Street.

The Masonic library is a treasure trove of Maine history, especially Civil War. But it's the temple's rooms that capture the imagination. With their vaulted ceilings, refined millwork, and exceptional detail, they live up to King Solomon's ideals, upon which the organization is founded.

Recently, Blue Elephant Catering combined forces with the Masons to host events in the wood-paneled Scottish Rite Reading Room and elegant Armory, topped with an original stained glass window of the Knights Templar. The rooms' architectural symbolsim would leave Nicolas Cage drooling for his next *National Treasure* clue.

415 Congress St.
portlandmasons.com
Blue Elephant Catering
207-281-3070
masonicblue.com

STAND NEXT TO BIGFOOT
AT THE INTERNATIONAL CRYPTOZOOLOGY MUSEUM

Loren Coleman claims that his collection of paraphernalia attributed to oddities, legends, and folklore is "the world's only cryptozoology museum," and that may very well be true. Where else could one see an "authentic fake" Feejee Mermaid? No, not Fiji. The film prop from *P.T. Barnum* is one of many artifacts and souvenirs exhibited.

Small in size, it's big in feet—the collection includes one hundred creatures' foot casts from sightings worldwide, and the museum's signature attraction and most popular photo op is an eight-foot-tall Bigfoot. The museum includes additional TV and film pieces, as well as the original artifact that started it all for Coleman: the burgee flag from the World Book's Snowman Expedition to the Himalayas led by Edmund Hillary and Marlin Perkins. Founded in 2003, the museum started in Coleman's private home and grew into its current downtown location just off Congress Street.

Whether it's due to the public's fascination with the unexplained, or *Time* magazine listing it as one of the "Ten Weirdest Museums in the World," or *Yankee* magazine picking it as one of the top five "Kid-Friendly Museums in New England," the International Cryptozoology Museum is getting discovered.

11 Avon St.
cryptozoologymuseum.com

PROHIBITION BIRTHPLACE
AT THE NEAL S. DOW MEMORIAL

Neal S. Dow was mayor of Portland, abolitionist, Civil War hero, and presidential candidate, but he is best known as the father of Prohibition. His Federal-style home tells all the tales.

While the Eighteenth Amendment prohibited the United States from the manufacture and sale of alcohol in 1919, this mayor of Portland secured statewide prohibition in 1851. This pioneering legislation became known as the Maine Law.

Founder of the Temperance Movement, his 1830 West End house is owned by the Maine Woman's Christian Temperance Union. By today's standards, Dow's amassed material is worthy of a *Hoarders* episode, but in a pre-digital age, it is a compelling and comprehensive record of a storied life. His furniture, books, papers, and even death mask—a three-dimensional cast of his face upon his demise—are available for viewing.

The Neal S. Dow Memorial estimates that there were "approximately three hundred establishments selling . . . alcoholic beverages along the roughly one mile stretch of Portland's major business district . . . during the first half of the 19th century." Oh, if only he could see it now!

714 Congress St,
207-773-7773
mewctu.org

PORTLAND RUM RIOTS

However sincere Neal S. Dow's motivations may have been, they were undermined by the Portland Rum Riots in 1855.

Dow attributed the rise in drunkenness to the Irish-immigrant seaport workers. The mayor's campaign was less xenophobic and more sociological. His papers and records relate how he was impacted by accounts of alcohol-related abuses and poverty he witnessed in Portland families.

An opposition political party discovered Dow's supply of alcohol stored for medicinal purposes. On the second anniversary of the Maine Law, tensions came to a head. Stirred up over the mayor's apparent hypocrisy, foreign-born citizens stormed city hall. Dow ordered the militia to fire into the mob, killing and wounding several people.

Found not guilty of violating his own law, his reputation was forever damaged politically, and he lost his bid for governor.

THE (OTHER) MONA LISA
AT PORTLAND MUSEUM OF ART

"If you went to Paris right now, you'll see the same thing," says Portland Museum of Art's Kristen Levesque of *La Gioconda*, a *Mona Lisa* look-a-like in the permanent collection. "It's been sent to Harvard's Straus Center for Conservation and Technical Studies for verification—painted in the same time period (before 1510) by a left-handed painter . . . just no signature to *prove* it!"

Indeed, Leonardo da Vinci's early-sixteenth-century portrait of a conspiratorial Lisa del Giocondo is the thing that dreams are made of. Like its autographed counterpart hanging in the Louvre since 1797, the PMA's Renaissance painting is also surprisingly small, measuring 64 cm × 54 cm (the *Mona Lisa* is 77 cm × 53 cm). Donated in 1983 by Prouts Neck resident Henry H. Reichhold, the unsigned *La Gioconda* doesn't often see the light of day. Due to its age and potential worth, the painting spends much of its time in the safety of the archives.

Unlike its Parisian doppelgänger, this *Da Vinci Code* goddess will be more approachable with shorter lines. Coming off its first major renovation in thirty years, the PMA has reintroduced this Italian dream girl to her fans for a prolonged appearance in the gallery. If not exhibited, viewings may be scheduled through requests in an Art Study Room.

7 Congress St.
207-775-6148
portlandmuseum.org

CONSPIRACY THEORISTS TAKE NOTE

Eerily, like Dan Brown's tale of intrigue, which involves da Vinci's famous *Mona Lisa* and the new I.M. Pei – designed wing of the Louvre Museum in Paris, *La Gioconda* in Portland is exhibited in an art museum with a contemporary addition also designed by I.M. Pei. Both paintings are in cities where French culture and art flourished. And Brown's fictional hero-expert is a professor at nearby Harvard, where the Portland painting has been authenticated. Coincidence?

It's no coincidence that the last time the painting was displayed for public viewing, *The Da Vinci Code* had just been released in theaters. The question is, was it an inspired marketing ploy or a calculated diversion? As Brown writes, "So dark the con of man."

• •

Each month, the PMA is open late for cocktails on the third Thursday, and for free on the first Friday. At both events the museum's galleries are accessible for viewing, including the *Mona Lisa* twin if on public display.

PORTLAND UNCHAINED
ON THE FREEDOM TRAIL

First, Portland's Freedom Trail has no relation to Boston's colonial-era struggle for freedom for the United States. The Forest City's trail exposes significant places that aided African Americans' freedom from within the United States. Currently, Maine Freedom Trails, Inc., maps thirteen marked sites "of sixteen that will constitute a permanent walking trail highlighting the people, places, events, and daily life associated with the Underground Railroad and anti-slavery movement in Portland."

The seaport's involvement with the Triangle Trade created conflicted sentiments in this northern state born from the Missouri Compromise. Sites include safe houses owned by active abolitionists; venues that hosted notable figures such as Susan B. Anthony, William Lloyd Garrison, and Frederick Douglass; locations of pro-slavery riots; and other significant links breaking the chains of slavery.

Given the period of the abolitionist movement, it's not surprising that most of the markers are congregated in the Old Port. Still, some markers seem to be missing. One notable absence is abolitionist Neal S. Dow's West End home—a known station on the Underground Railroad. In the party of President Abraham Lincoln, a missing link recognizing the Republican mayor's home is odd.

Beginning at the floor of Franklin St.
207-591-9980
portlandfreedomtrail.org

PORTLAND FREEDOM TRAIL SITES

1. Franklin Street Wharf, Casco Bay Lines
2. Barber Shop of Jacob C. Dickson, 243 Fore Street
3. Hack Stand of Charles H. L. Pierre, 29 Middle Street
4. Abyssinian Meeting House, 73 Newbury Street
5. Home of Charles Frederick, Harriet Stephenson Eastman, and Alexander Stephenson, corner of Mountfort and Newbury Streets
6. Eastern Cemetery, corner of Congress and Mountfort Streets
7. Home of Elias and Elizabeth Widgery Thomas, corner of India and Congress Streets
8. Home of General Samuel C. Fessenden, 31 India Street
9. Friends (Quaker) Meeting House, Lincoln Park, corner of Federal and Pearl Streets
10. Hack Stand of Reuben Ruby, corner of Federal and Temple Streets
11. First Parish Unitarian Universalist Church, 425 Congress Street
12. Secondhand Clothing Store of Lloyd Scott, 44 Exchange Street
13. Mariners' Church, Corner of Fore and Market Streets

HOME STREET ADVANTAGE
ON BOWDOIN STREET

Turn-of-the-century architect John Calvin Stevens developed architectural styles in Portland as influential as his Midwestern contemporary Frank Lloyd Wright. Inspired by New England– and Victorian-style buildings, Stevens pioneered the Shingle and Colonial Revival styles that quickly swept the northeast. While Stevens is credited with over a thousand buildings in Maine, Bowdoin Street off the Western Promenade presents a cluster of his best work, including his own 1882 self-designed home at number 52.

"In time, Bowdoin Street became itself a monument to Stevens and his architectural style," writes John F. Bauman in *Gateway to Vacationland: The Making of Portland, Maine*. Indeed, the short Bowdoin Street is a love letter to Stevens, or rather, a collection of his affectionate missives to Portland. Made with wood, brick, and stone, the houses vary in style as much as they do materials. While his Shingle style is well represented on Bowdoin Street, Stevens's Colonial Revival brick mansion built for lawyer Richard Webb in 1907 at the corner of Vaughan Street anchors the architect's presence.

If the West End street whets the architectural appetite for John Calvin Stevens, there are almost three hundred more buildings to see scattered throughout the city. Another option is to go to the waterfront offices of SMRT—the firm he founded—and hire his great-grandson Paul to design one.

Spans between Western Promenade and Neal St.
portlandlandmarks.org

JOHN CALVIN STEVENS BOWDOIN STREET HOMES

6 Bowdoin St., Richard Edward H. Davies House, 1890

9 Bowdoin St., Nathan Clifford House, 1902; alterations for William M. Bradley, 1906

28 Bowdoin St., Franklin C. Pyson House, 1901

29 Bowdoin St., Richard Webb House, 1907

36 Bowdoin St., Henry L. Houghton House, 1887

40 Bowdoin St., Lucius M. Clark House, 1887-88

41 Bowdoin St., Charles D. Alexander Garage, 1917

44 Bowdoin St., Montgomery S. Hibson House, 1885-86

52 Bowdoin St., John Calvin Stevens House, 1882

55 Bowdoin St., Harrison J. Holt House, 1911

56 Bowdoin St., William H. Dennett House, 1884

62 Bowdoin St., John H. Davis House, 1883

71 Bowdoin St., Herbert Payson House, 1906-7

Information compiled from: *John Calvin Stevens on the Portland Peninsula, 1880 to 1940*, by Earle G. Shettleworth Jr., and https://pinterest.com/mainehistory/john-calvin-stevens

KID AROUND
AT THE CHILDREN'S MUSEUM & THEATRE

Located in the Arts District of downtown Portland, the Children's Museum & Theatre of Maine features a wide variety of interactive exhibits and activities for children and families. Fly a space shuttle, spin the world, visit foreign countries and learn about other cultures, pet a starfish, climb a rock wall, fight a fire, captain a pirate ship or lobster boat, or just play in a tree house. Beyond that, the theater presents live performances for children, with children, and by children! Acting, audition, and improv classes are offered free of charge on scheduled days.

142 Free St.
207-828-1234
kitetails.org

SHOPPING AND FASHION

SHOP 'TIL YOU DRINK
AT MERRY MADNESS

Give into the (Merry) Madness and eat, drink, and shop downtown all night long on the second Thursday of December. The evening kicks off at a city hotel (it rotates annually) where revelers pay $15 to get in the holiday spirit by eating delicious bites from local eateries, enjoying live music, participating in a silent auction, and receiving a commemorative glass with wine, beer, or coffee. From there, festive holiday shoppers spill into the streets to explore participating downtown stores that are open until 10 p.m., often refreshing their glasses with free refills (tequila shots, anyone?) at stores along the way. Sales, street performers, carolers, free samples, and giddy gatherings keep the merriment moving.

Sponsored by Portland's Downtown District, this annual tradition is Portland's opportunity to reintroduce the joys of shopping in the city.

Portland's Downtown District
549 Congress St.
207-772-6828
portlandmaine.com

BLACK FRIDAY
ON MOONLIGHT MADNESS

For an old-school way to shop on Black Friday, step aboard for a bit of nostalgic elegance when the Amtrak Downeaster pulls out of the Portland Transportation Center station at 10:05 p.m. on Thanksgiving night.

For only $5, the quick trip brings eager holiday shoppers to Freeport— imagine Fifth Avenue in a Rockwell-style village. Hot cocoa, entertainment, and activities greet the train's arrival.

Because of Freeport's strict zoning, the walkable town looks like a quiet New England village, which includes stores like Coach, The North Face, Burberry, Oakley, Ralph Lauren Polo, Abercrombie & Fitch, and others. Even the downtown McDonalds is in a country farmhouse—not made to look like one, a *real* one! The sales start at midnight, and the stores practically pay *you* to shop!

Portland Transportation Center
100 Thompson's Point Road
800-872-7245
amtrakdowneaster.com/black-friday-fares

Town of Freeport
freeportusa.com

Impatient spendthrifts or window shoppers can still venture into L.L. Bean when the train arrives. This is world headquarters for the famed outdoor retailer, and the doors on all the campus stores have no locks because they *never close*. Their 24/7/365 business model was grandfathered in decades earlier.

THE GIFT OF PORTLAND
AT SPRINGER'S JEWELERS

Iconic landmarks have been treasured holiday gifts in downtown Portland since 1988.

New designs are created every year for the family-run Springer's Jewelers and fabricated into a three-dimensional 18K gold-plated brass ornament. Made in the USA, these collectible keepsakes are an annual tradition for locals celebrating Christmastime in their city, snowbirds missing home, or visitors looking to mark the year with a memorable talisman.

"Casco Bay Lines ferry is our most popular, *by far*," says Springer's longtime employee Kathi Adams. "The initial order for a thousand was all gone before Christmas! We had to scramble to get more in on time. People love it."

Multidimensional ornaments successfully represent the chosen subject. In recent years, splashes of color were added, including the white and yellow hull of the Casco Bay Lines Ferries (2006), red doors of First Parish Unitarian Universalist Church (2007), and green grass at Hadlock Field (2008).

580 Congress Street
800-725-5404
springersjewelers.com

As the annual ornaments enter their third decade, Portland City Hall (1994) is the first to be retired and no longer available. Alert eBay!

SHOP FARM-TO-TABLE
AT THE OLDEST FARMERS' MARKET
IN NEW ENGLAND

Every Saturday morning, spring through late fall, foodies and gardeners descend on Deering Oaks Park. They shop for the freshest ingredients, flowers, plants, and crafts Maine has to offer . . . that week. Every Wednesday, a similar ritual of commerce occurs amid the high-rises of Monument Square. In the cold weather months, the market moves to an indoor location in East Bayside. For two and a half centuries, Portland's farmers' market has continuously been bringing fresh farm produce, meat, plants, and crafts to its urban center and many of the best restaurants. Being part of that tradition is a bit humbling.

Shortly before the revolution in 1768, Portland—then known as Falmouth—established a public market in the town hall to regulate the food being sold by rural farmers. After the revolution, the city (renamed Portland) made Market Square (now Monument Square) home to the farmers' market. Consistently rated one of the top markets in the United States, it's almost as important socially as it is commercially. Family and friends schedule their days around it, some making it a weekly gathering.

Deering Oaks Park, Saturdays, 7 a.m.–1 p.m., May-November
200 Anderson Street, Saturdays, 9 a.m.–1 p.m., December-April
Monument Square, Wednesdays, 7 a.m.–1 p.m.
portlandmainefarmersmarket.org

HAVE A BROMANCE
AT MENSROOM

Men who are dumbfounded by the cost of women's hairstyling will be perplexed no more—or at least will have a deeper appreciation after this guilty pleasure in the Mensroom. The innovative man-cave salon can make even the most alpha male betray his $10 haircut barber. Tuesday's two-for-one haircut and style may also have them redefine date night as well, when bringing a buddy cuts the price in half.

Entering the exposed-brick shop, long-haired patrons are greeted by a smiling hostess who offers complimentary coffee, wine, or beer. A window-side table overlooks Monument Square and a leather couch and recliners surround a large flat-screen, often televising news or sports. A dartboard and pool table offer active distractions while waiting for an appointment.

When it's time, stylists lead their clientele away to plush chairs, beginning by sloughing off stress with a shoulder and head massage. The relaxation continues as a heated towel envelops the face with selected scents while hair is washed and conditioned. Artistically styled, the final touches leave customers feeling fresh and fully rejuvenated.

If not, there's always time for another game of eight ball.

8 City Center
207-874-8080
mensroomsalon.com

HEY, ISN'T THAT BARNEY STINTSON OVER THERE? Beyond a haircut, the pampered male can also get skin care, manicures, pedicures, shaves, facials, hair waxes, and perhaps camo color to blend the gray hair that isn't there. Just don't tell the guys at poker night . . . unless they're already here.

TOP OUT
AT QUEEN OF HATS

Regardless of whether customers are attending a summer wedding, Easter Sunday services, the Kentucky Derby, a day at the beach, or are just fashionistas, they pay homage to the Queen of Hats. Dorinda Putnam's Arts District shop has the perfect chapeau for every occasion.

Shortly after the ball drops at midnight on New Year's Eve, Putnam begins blocking out hats through the winter to be ready for the warm weather rush. Beyond the ladies who come to the store to pick up their extravagant Kentucky Derby hats, the designer ships a couple dozen to Louisville for the Run for the Roses. Then summer comes . . .

"Between weddings and the beach, we're selling out of my designs in the summer—nothing left!" says Putnam. "I'm seeing the license plates— New York, Massachusetts, Pennsylvania—more out-of-state people are discovering us!"

Beyond Putnam's creations, Queen of Hats offers headwear from top designers. The upscale selection at Queen of Hats may be perceived as expensive, but it's a great value if it makes you look like a million bucks.

560 Congress St.
888-373-0602
queenofhats.com

Popular cloche hats sell well in Portland "because 1920s-style is hot now and they're close to the head," Putnam advises. "On the Maine coast, wide-brim hats gets caught in the wind. They're like big sails here—*whoosh*, they're gone! Fascinators are good, too."

CHARMING PORTLAND
WITH CHART METALWORKS

"Casco Bay is the most popular design with out-of-state customers—it encompasses the largest area of Portland," says Charlotte Guptill of her jewelry line's navigation-chart accents. CHART Metalworks exploded on the scene in 2006 when avid sailor Guptill, after abandoning a career as a loan officer, began to incorporate snippets of nautical maps into pendants being created in her fledgling business. The in-demand Casco Bay collection features pewter and sterling silver pieces cast in Maine, accented with adornments of tiny charts highlighting Portland's waterfront. Charts depict the downtown peninsula with Back Bay, Casco Bay, and the Calendar Islands, as well as a map of the entire state. Drawing inspiration from their boating theme, CHART Metalworks recently introduced bronze. Known by sailors to never rust or tarnish, the metal forms a lovely patina over time.

The jewelry line now includes earrings, bracelets, and accessories—even cufflinks and other menswear. "Our biggest sellers are key rings," smiles Guptill. "They're one size fits all, and appeal to young and old, men and women."

From their studio overlooking a statue of Portland native John Ford, custom orders nationwide have evolved to include inland maps. Like the famous director outside, Guptill knows how to convey a map of the human heart.

1 Pleasant St.
207-221-6807
chartmetalworks.com

COME SAIL AWAY
AT SEA BAGS

"All our bags are made from recycled sails," says Sea Bags employee Justin Holdefer about the fashion-forward tote. "If you bring in a sail, we'll make your bag for free based on its size."

The Custom House Wharf company's innovative twist on the working waterfront encourages customers to design bags to fit their personality. Each item is hand-stitched to ensure quality and uniqueness—"each bag is truly one of a kind." Bags are brandished as fashion statements and spotted by locals miles away.

Sails are also turned into various sized bags, luggage tags, and wine totes. For customers who'd rather stick with traditional designs, "The Navy Anchor design is our most popular tote right now," says Holdefer. "The Octopus Tote lined with Charles Darwin's notes is also a big seller."

24 Custom House Wharf
207-780-0744
seabags.com

KEEP IT SIMPLE
WITH JILL McGOWAN

"I started . . . with two guiding principles: to create beautiful clothing that is comfortable and fashionable, and to make clothing of quality that will endure fashion changes and wear well," says Jill McGowan. Launched in 1994, the clean lines and durable craftsmanship of her elegant all-cotton white shirts resonated with women, uncovering an unexpectedly high-end niche. The designer quickly garnered attention from fashion magazines and other media, including a heralded visit from Martha Stewart. Her intown studio was flooded with orders from retailers nationwide. Jill McGowan clothing is now sold nationwide and makes cameo appearances on television and in films. But the native Mainer still calls Portland home.

McGowan has since deviated from simple white blouses, but stays true to her vision. Still American made, fabrics include knits and blends. Designs also venture into patterns, textures, and even a color palette. Other garments make bolder statements, trading the traditional white for strong red, blue, or black solids. McGowan's casual line, 94 Portland, is more adventurous, with whimsical patterns playing off an even broader spectrum of color. But don't be fooled—white is *still* the new black.

Studio: 45 Casco St.
207-772-2199
jillmcgowan.com

Flagship store: 56 Main St.
Freeport
207-865-0909

SUGGESTED
ITINERARIES

COUPLES

CREATIVES

FAMILIES

URBANITES

Bintliff's American Café, 36
Blue, 61
Bramhall Pub, 32
Grace Restaurant, 7
Harvest on the Harbor, 16
Holy Donut, 34
Ice Bar, 30
Jay York Concerts, 45
LFK Burger, 31
Marcy's Diner, 40
Mensroom, 132
Merry Madness, 128
MJ's Wine Bar, 28
Old Port, 64

Portland Club, 72
Portland Harbor Hotel, 30
Portland Regency Hotel & Spa, 33
Queen of Hats, 133
St. Lawrence Arts, 45
State Theatre, 57
Thirsty Pig, 13
Tiaras & Tonic at Vena's Fizz
   House, 27
Top of the East, 3
Western Promenade, 50
Westin Portland Harborview Hotel, 3
Wharf Street, 46

QUIET SEEKERS

Diamond's Edge Restaurant &
   Marina, 21
Eastern Promenade, 52
First Parish Church, 59
Fore River Sanctuary, 90
Fort Allen Park, 108
Fort Gorges, 88
Maine Sailing Adventures, 14
Mail Boat Run, 66
Maine Jewish Museum, 105

MJ's Wine Bar, 28
Peaks Island, 58
Portland Club, 72
Portland Head Light, 94
Portland Trails, 76
Wadsworth-Longfellow House
   & Garden, 110
West End, 100
Western Cemetery, 115

SPENDTHRIFTS & WINDOW SHOPPERS

Amtrak Downeaster Moonlight
   Madness, 129
Freeport, 129
L.L. Bean, 129
Mensroom, 132

Old Port, 64
Queen of Hats, 133
Sea Bags, 135
Springer's Jewelers, 130

NIGHT OWLS

Bubba's Sulky Lounge, 48
J's Oyster, 8
L.L. Bean, 129
Novare Res, 42

Pizza Villa, 25
State Theatre, 57
Top of the East, 3

AUTHENTIC MAINE

Cape Elizabeth Light, 95
East End Beach, 83
Eastern Promenade, 52
Farmer's Market, 131
First Parish Church, 59
Fore River Sanctuary, 90
Fort Allen Park, 108
Fort Gorges, 88
J's Oyster, 8
Lucky Catch Cruises, 65

Maine Sailing Adventures, 14
Portland Trails, 76
Wadsworth-Longfellow House
  & Garden, 110
West End, 100
Western Cemetery, 115
Western Promenade, 50
Wharf Street, 46
Winslow Homer's Studio, 93

ACTIVITIES
BY SEASON

WINTER

'80s Night, 48
Altrusa's Great Chili & Chowder Challenge, 9
Blue, 61
Bramhall Pub, 32
Fore Street Restaurant, 24
Garlic Chicken Pie at Pizza Villa, 25
Horse-Drawn Carriage Rides, 64
Ice Bar at Portland Harbor Hotel, 30
J's Oyster, 8
La Gioconda at PMA, 120
Magic of Christmas at PSO, 54
Merry Madness, 128

MJ's Wine Bar, 28
New Year's Eve Black & White Soiree at Victoria Mansion, 106
Nordic Skiing, 76
Parade of Lights, 75
Polar Bear Dip & Dash, 83
Portland Club Billiards, 72
St. Lawrence Arts, 45
Springer's Jewelers Christmas Ornament, 130
Tiaras & Tonic at Vena's Fizz House, 27

SPRING

DiMillo's on the Water, 4
Easter Sunrise Service at Fort Allen Park, 108
First Parish Church Noonday Concerts, 7
Fore River Sanctuary at Jewell Falls, 90
Freedom Trail, 122
Grace Restaurant, 7
Hot Suppa' for Eggs Benedict, 26
International Cryptozoology Museum, 117
Italian Sandwiches at Amato's, 29
Langlais Art Trail, 102
Maine Jewish Museum, 105
Maine State Basketball Championship, 80

Marley, Bob, 55
Masonic Temple, 116
Mensroom, 132
Mr. Bagel (Downtown), 20
Neal S. Dow Memorial, 118
Old Port Festival, 56
Porthole Restaurant & Pub All-You-Can-Eat Fish & Chips, 18
Portland Fire Museum Horses, 99
Queen of Hats, 133
Rainy Day Room at Wadsworth-Longfellow House & Garden, 110
Rappel a High-Rise for Rippleffect, 81
Shipyard Brewing Company, 22
State Theatre Concerts, 57

INDEX